MENTOR TO RICHES

100 Hidden Secrets to Make Money on the Internet

Lots of ideas and methods you need

To know to start making money on

The Internet

By

MD Salah Elsayed

In most cases no start up money is needed

This book is dedicated to every man and woman who

have been affected by the recent economic downturn.

I hope this book will be of help to each one of them.

It is also dedicated to my wife and daughter who stood

with me during the birth of this book.

Contents

Introduction: --- 15

Chapter 1: --- 17

An idea for your Web Site

Chapter 2: --- 19

A name for your web site

Chapter 3: --- 21

A Home to your Web Site

Chapter 4: --- 23

Web Site Design

Chapter 5: --- 27

Web Site Development

Chapter 6: --- 30

E-Commerce

Chapter 7: --- 33

Web Site Optimization

Chapter 8: --- 35

Search Engine Optimization

Chapter 9: -- 38

Internet Marketing

Chapter 10: --- 45

Making money with your Web Site

Chapter 11: --- 47

EBay the King of the Jungle

Chapter 12: --- 52

Other Internet auctions

Chapter13: -- 55

Better than an auction

Chapter 14: --- 58

Cash for used Books

Chapter 15: --- 64

Sell on PriceGrabber.Com

Chapter 16: --- 70

Selling Digital Information

Chapter 17: --- 74

Making money with E-Books

Chapter 18: --- 78

Making money with Online Self Publishing

Chapter 19: --- 83

Your own Blog

Chapter 20: --- 87

Podcasting for Cash

Chapter 21: --- 91

RSS Feed

Chapter 22: --- 93

Starting a Wiki

Chapter 23: --- 96

Selling Domains

Chapter 24: --- 100

Selling Web Sites

Chapter 25: --- 102

PayPal

Chapter 26: --- 105

Google Checkout

Chapter 27: -- 106

Making Money by Saving Money

Chapter 28: -- 108

Freebies

Chapter 29: -- 110

Making Money with Online Jobs

Chapter 30: -- 112

Making Money with affiliation Programs

Chapter 31: -- 114

Making Money with Unclaimed Property

Chapter 32: -- 117

A Web Site for a Non Profit

Chapter 33: -- 119

Directory of Import Export Web Site

Chapter 34: -- 121

Doing Business Somewhere Web Site

Chapter 35: -- 123

Outsourcing Web Site

Chapter 36: -- 125

Best of the Best Directory Web Site

Chapter 37: -- 127

Making Money Web Site

Chapter 38: -- 129

Saving Money Web Site

Chapter 39: -- 131

How to Web Site

Chapter 40: -- 133

Business Startups Web Site

Chapter 41: -- 135

A Web Site for Health Issues

Chapter 42: -- 137

Go Wireless Web Site

Chapter 43: -- 139

Search Engine Optimization Web Site

Chapter 44: -- 141

Digital Photography Web Site

Chapter 45: -- 143

IVF Web Site

Chapter 46: -- **145**

Video Conference Web Site

Chapter 47: -- **147**

Kits to go Web Site

Chapter 48: -- **149**

Domains Web Site

Chapter 49: -- **151**

New Products Web Site

Chapter 50: -- **153**

Business Ideas Web Site

Chapter 51: -- **155**

Going Green Web Site

Chapter 52: -- **157**

Go Solar Web Site

Chapter 53: -- **159**

Wind Energy Web Site

Chapter 54: -- **161**

The Antique E-shop

Chapter 55: --- 163

Testing New Products Web Site

Chapter 56: --- 165

A Web Site for Consulting

Chapter 57: --- 167

Corporate Gossip Web Site

Chapter 58: --- 168

Helping Hand Web Site

Chapter 59: --- 169

Distressed Businesses Web Site

Chapter 60: --- 171

Special Group Interests Web Site

Chapter 61: --- 173

The Rich & Famous Web Site

Chapter 62: --- 175

The Rise of a great Company Web Site

Chapter 63: --- 177

Specific Technology Web Site

Chapter 64: -- 179

Specific Industry Web Site

Chapter 65: -- 181

A Web Site for a Specific Country

Chapter 66: -- 183

A Web Site for a specific Star

Chapter 67: -- 185

Membership Web Site

Chapter 69: -- 187

Before you Go Web Site

Chapter 70: -- 189

Seniors Web Site

Chapter 71: -- 191

Stressed out Web Site

Chapter 72: -- 193

Free Things Web Site

Chapter 73: -- 195

Education Web Site

Chapter 74: --- 199

Colleges Web Site

Chapter 75: --- 201

Information Web Site

Chapter 76: --- 203

Recycling Web Site

Chapter 77: --- 205

A Web Site for Women

Chapter 78: --- 207

Presentations Web Site

Chapter 79: --- 209

Writing Skills Web Site

Chapter 80: --- 211

Making Money with Business Networking Sites

Chapter 81: --- 214

Making Money with Video Sharing Sites

Chapter 82: --- 217

Making Money with Social Networking Sites

Chapter 83: --- 220

Making Money with Google

Chapter 84: -- 223

Making Money with Yahoo

Chapter 85: -- 225

Making Money with Microsoft

Chapter 86: -- 227

A Graphic Design Web Site

Chapter 87: -- 229

Federal Programs Web Site

Chapter 88: -- 230

Making Money with Amazon

Chapter 89: -- 232

Making Money with Content Driven Web Sites

Chapter 90: -- 235

Making Money with Elance.Com

Chapter 91: -- 240

Making Money with Craigslist

Chapter 92: -- 243

Making Money with Free Classifieds

Chapter 93: -- 245

Making Money with your Online Store

Chapter 94: -- 247

Making Money with Free Online Stores

Chapter 95: -- 248

Making Money with ClickBank.com

Chapter 96: -- 254

Making Money with RentAcoder.Com

Chapter 97: -- 259

VOIP Web Site

Chapter 98: -- 261

Web Site for Network Security

Chapter 99: -- 263

Web Site for Security Systems

Chapter 100: -- 264

Today's Funny Web Site

Conclusion: -- 266

Introduction

I wrote this book for anyone who wants to make money online and serious about it. For the most part, I tried to steer clear of the technical details like programming and code editing. This is not what this book is for. I discussed in this book ideas, concepts and methods that you can try to make more money on the Internet. You need to build up on these ideas and methods. What you will take from reading this book is up to you. At the very least, it will give you something to think about and may open up the opportunity for improvement, action and seriousness.

How this book is organized:

I tried to layout this book and organize it in 100 chapters. Each chapter is discussing a new idea or a way that can help you get started in one way or another and start make the money you need.

Who should read this book:

Practically anyone who is looking to make money will benefit from reading this book, no matter how much knowledge he or she has and no matter how much money he or she has. When I wrote this book I had two groups of people on my mind. The first group of people are those who do not have a lot of computer knowledge, do not have a lot of start up money, do not have a web site, are not willing to have a web site and are only looking for some extra cash e.g. few hundreds to few thousand dollars a month. A lot of chapters are dedicated to this group of people. They do not have to go through the whole book. The second group of people are those who have some computer knowledge and are willing to go all the way. These people already have a web site or are willing to have one. They are looking to make a lot of money.

My advice to both groups is to focus on one or two things at a time. If you try to do everything at one time, you will end up doing nothing. Read the whole book first then pick up something you like; something that makes sense to you.

I tried to put a lot of details but I am limited to the size of the book and a lot of details is beyond the scope of this book. So, my advice to you once you pick up the right thing is to collect as much information as you can. I tried to provide you with a lot of resources so you can do a lot of research because as they always say, the devil is in the details. However, I do not want you to take weeks or months to research. Act fast and do not waste a lot of resources. Time is money. Invest in your project as little money as you can because you do not know whether it is going to work for you or not. Once you are sure you are doing fine and you start making money, it is time to expand cautiously.

After you read this book:

After you've had read this book at least once and you would like to send me a comment or a question you are welcome to contact me directly via e-mail at consultme4less@yahoo.com. I do my best to answer your inquiry.

Chapter 1

An Idea for Your Web Site

Welcome to the World Wide Web. If you are looking to be rich and famous , you came to the right place. Now you decided to have your own web site. For the purpose of this book, your web site is supposed to make you money. After deciding to have your own web site, your next step is supposed to have an idea for that web site. This is the most important piece of the puzzle. I can't stress how essential this step is. It is the difference between success and failure. When looking for an idea to your web site, you to consider two important points. The first point is whether your idea is going to sell. The second point is how much competition is out there. I will discuss both points in details.

Ideas that can sell:

A lot of times, when starting a new business, most of the experts will tell you to start a business in something you like or you have passion for. The truth is that many times what you like can not sell. If it doesn't sell you are in trouble. So, the general rule is to look for something that can sell. If it happens that you like it, that means you will more successful in it. Make a long list of what you think are good ideas. Go through this book and pick up the ideas you like. Ask friends and do a lot of research because this step will make or break your business. Once you make your list of ideas, it is time to check which one is going to sell. There are lots of web sites that measure the amount of traffic concerning any of these searches. This will tell you whether there is a high demand for any of these ideas or not. Some of the web sites that can help you with this are: http://www.inventortoverture.com   and http://www.goodkeywords.com.

There are others, just go to online and do a search on " Search Analytics ". It is your job to get that part right. Web search analytics is a big subject that is beyond the scope of this book.

Competition:

Sometimes you come up with a great idea that has a big market but you have one problem. That problem is the fact that there is a lot of competition. A lot of competition is not good for you because these sites usually have more resources than you do. A mild competition is usually healthy and it tells you that your idea has a market. It is very easy to spot the level of competition you are going to have. Just do an online search and look at the result of your search. Generally, if your idea is broad, expect to face a very tough competition. You will be competing with big guys and you can't win. Try to narrow your idea as much as you can. I give you an example. Suppose you want to have a retail site selling shoes. You will be having no chance of success because there are already thousands of web sites selling shoes, most of them have much more resources than you do. If you try to narrow your idea and decide to sell only women shoes, your idea is still broad enough and your chance of success is still no good. If you make another try and decide to sell old women shoes, your idea is still too broad. If you specialize in selling shoes to old women who have foot problems, you might be able to make it. Still it might be better if you can narrow your idea even further. Hopefully by now you understand what I mean by targeting a small group of audience who are interested in your idea.

Sometimes you come up with an idea that has a huge market, a market that is big enough to accommodate everybody. It is like a matter of supply and demand. If the demand for your idea is too high and the supply is too low, you still have a chance of success, but you have to act fast before the market becomes oversaturated, then you will be in trouble.

Another time, you come up with a new idea that has no market at all. If you think it is a promising idea that will have a lot of audience, you can go ahead and create a new market for it. But this will be too much for a little guy like you. Even if you succeed in creating a new market for your new idea, very soon it will be copied before you can make any money out of it. So, my advice is to stay away from this last one.

Now you come up with a good idea that has a good market and you do not have a lot of competition, you still have more work to do. You need to explore your competitors' web sites to have an idea about what they are doing. Ask yourself that question: " What can I do more to gain the competitive advantage? ". What I mean by competitive advantage is that you need to do some more than your competitors so you can take over the market and attract more customers. This can take many forms. For example, you can offer a better customer service. You can offer lower prices. You can offer products of higher or better quality. There are a lot of great ideas that you can use to achieve this goal. It is very important to have the competitive advantage over your competitors.

Now, let us move to the next step in building your own web site.

Chapter 2

A Name for Your Web Site

You do not want me to explain to you what a domain is because I think you already know. You need a good domain for your web site. A good domain is very important to the success of your web site business. The question is: "What makes a good domain? ". A good domain should have something to do with your web site activities. If you are selling something, your domain should tell your customers that you are selling that thing e.g. http://www.software.com. This domain tells the customers that this web site is dealing with software. A good domain should be very easy to spell, the shorter, the better e.g. http://www.shop.com. A good domain should be very easy to pronounce. This will make it possible to pass it by telephone from one friend to the other. One word domains are gone long time ago and they are selling for thousands and even millions of dollars these days. Domain names are like real estates. A lot of people who have good vision, went on and registered hundreds of these good domains long time ago. They made this as a sort of investment and so far it has proven to be the best investment ever. They are now selling them and making lots of money. Your only hope now is for a two word domain, though it will not come easily. If your domain is made up of two words, you need to avoid double letters. Avoid the combinations of two words that have the same letter repeated at the end of the first word and at the beginning of the second word e.g. http://www.shoppinggoods.com. Make sure your domain name can be easily remembered. A very good way to buy a domain at a reasonable price is through the eBay auction site. I saw a lot of good domains listed for auction at a very reasonable price. You can grab one of these. It looks to me that some people registered a lot of domains, much more than they can handle or sell, and they turn around selling them on eBay for a modest profit. There is one strategy that I used to get all of my good domains. I made a very long list of possible good names. I always have a pen and a piece of paper in my pocket for that reason. Once a possible good name comes to my mind I immediately write it down. When I go home I go to one of these web sites that are specialized in registering domains, take my list out of my pocket and check the availability of each one of them. Once I find an available domain, I register it immediately. You can use the same strategy to acquire as many good domains as you can for building new web sites or for sale. Believe me, it is a good investment if you acquire the good ones.

A domain name is so important to your online business that you can spend even weeks to get the right one.

Chapter 3

A Home To Your Web Site

A web site has to be on a server that is connected to the Internet all the time. This is called web site hosting. When it comes to web site hosting, you have two choices. The first choice is to host your web site on your own server. This is an expensive choice unless you have the resources, you have the technical skills and you are doing a big project. If you do it this way, you will have a better control over your web site. This is what most of the big companies and big businesses are doing. On the individual level you still can do the same thing. You will need a high speed connection and you need to build your own server. Building your own server can be expensive in terms of hardware and software. Your server should be connected to the Internet all the time. The second choice is what most of the people usually do. Simply, they look for a hosting company. There are thousands of them all over the place and the competition is tough, so the prices for hasting are going way down. I am not going to recommend a special hosting company for you. There are lots of good hosting companies over there. When choosing a hosting company do not make your decision just on the price or fees. Look at what they offer. Technical support is very important especially for those with little computer skills. Good customer service is a very essential matter, you need someone who does not ignore you. You need someone who responds to your requests fast. When it comes to fees, some of them have what is called setup fees, usually it is waived by some companies for a special period of time. Almost all of these companies offer different levels of hosting. Every level has its own fees. If you pay your fees annually you save money. The best deals are usually available with a one year contract or more. They want to keep you as a customer.

If you expect your web site to take off and you will get a lot of visitors you should check the traffic limits i.e. how much traffic the company will allow you to have. This is called bandwidth. Bandwidth is very important especially for those web sites dealing with downloadable audio, video, games, software etc. These are huge files and they eat up a lot of bandwidth. It will nice to find a company that offer no limits when it comes to bandwidth, but I do not think you will be able to find one. If you are going to have a lot of audio and video files in your web site, you should check how much storage capacity you will be allowed. Audio and video files take a lot of storage space. There should be other services and tools that are included in the deal. You should check them out and compare with other companies before you sign up. I recommend that you sign up for one month first to test the water and see how things are going. If everything is fine and you feel you are getting your money worth then you can sign up for a one year contract. It is not a good idea to jump from one hosting company to the other because it is not an easy process. So do your homework first.

One other important point is that some people just go and sign up with a hosting company before even doing anything like building his web site. Build your own web site first and have it ready to be published then go and contract with a hosting company because , depending on the complexity of your project and your skills, it might take you months before you have your web site ready to publish.

Chapter 4

Web Site Design

Before you start building up your web site you have to design it on papers first. You need to design each page of your site separately. A web site is made up of the main home page and other pages that are linked together in one way or another. The main home page is like the store front and is linked to all the pages in your web site.

When it comes to web site design, you need to make sure that your web site will be easy to download. Since graphics and animations do not download fast, a word of caution is to use graphics and multimedia only when it is necessary. Your audience expects your site to download fast. Should your web site takes time to download, your customers will go somewhere else and probably will never come back.

Another point is that your site should be easy to navigate and rich in content. This is very important because most of us who go online go there looking for good usable information.

Your home page:

Your home page is the primary gate to your web site. You should spend as much time as you can to make it as perfect as possible. Your home page is the most important part of your web site. This is the first page that your potential customers see. If they like it they will continue navigating the other pages. If your home page does not give a good impression, your customers will go away and may never come back again. My advice to you is that before you start designing your home page, go visit other web sites, look at the overall design, look at the layout and the elements that are included. Study all the details of the home pages of your competitors. You need to have a pen and a piece of paper and write down the positive elements you saw and would like to include in your web site. There are a lot of elements that you should include in your home page. Your company's name and your company's logo should be at the top and the bottom of your home page. If you do not have a logo for your company try to design one yourself. Even a very primitive logo is better than nothing at all. It gives your customers the impression that they are dealing with a big and professional business. Your company's name and logo should also be included in every other web page. It is very important to also include your company's contact information in your home page as well as every other page. The contact information usually goes at the bottom. The contact information can enhance your company's image, credibility and can create a lot of confidence among your customers. They will believe that they dealing with a legitimate business. Your contact information can be in the form of an address, phone number or email. The company's email is a must because you can expect that most of the customers' contacts will be through the email. Every company should have a privacy policy. A link to the company's privacy policy should be included at the bottom of the home page. You should also include links to all other pages from your main home page. With a click of a button, your customers can go to any page in your web site. This can be done by including a menu on the side of the page or a navigation bar at the top . If you designing your site to be a retail site and you have different products to sell, try to put them in categories on the left side of your main home page. If you are offering a daily or weekly specials or any kinds of promotions, add a link to it. That link is better done with a picture or some kind of animation to draw the attention of the customer. If you are planning a huge web site, you will be better off adding a search box. Your customers will appreciate it when they can find exactly what they are looking for just by typing few words and click the go button. This arrangement can put you head to head with the big guys. It will enhance your image and make you look professional. It will nice if you add a mission statement that spells your activity in an attractive way using something like animation. For example, if you are selling cable, your statement should be something like this : " We are selling hard to find cables at a discount price ".

This is about your main home page. What about the other pages ? The other pages that should be included are:

Product pages:

If you are building a retail web site, you will have products to sell. Each product should have its own separate page. It should include a full description of the item. Put as much detail as you can with pictures because the buyer relies on this information to make his decision. Also, you need to mention the price. Also include " add to cart" button.

Shopping Cart Page:

I will talk about shopping cart with more details later. For now, the shopping cart is part of your payment system. When customers are ready to order one or more of your products, they click on " Buy Now " or " order " button which takes them to your site's shopping cart. Your shopping cart should have the ability to accept coupons and discounts.

Return Policy Page:

If you want your customers to their shopping at your site and come back later, you should have a return policy. With no doubt, this will increase the sales volume because your customers will have a lot of confidence in your site.

Promotions page:

In this page you can practice your marketing skills. This is where you promote your business. It can include coupons, discounts, prizes and so on.

FAQ Page:

FAQ stands for Frequently Asked Questions. This page will save time and headache for both you and your customers. You need to design this page to have the answers for most of the questions that you expect your customers to ask. Imagine yourself as a customer and make a list of the possible questions and fully answer them .

Customers' Testimonials Page:

This page will create even more confidence among your customers as soon as they read some of the testimonials in this page. You can ask your customer to write their comments about their shopping experiences in a form or they can submit their comments by email. Few times you may receive an offensive comment, you just ignore it. You need to mention only the positive comments.

About us page:

This page is almost included in every web site. It is nothing but a summary about the company, its mission, goals and activities.

Help, customer service or technical support page:

Whatever you call it, the goal is the same, to help your customers have a nice shopping experience. If you want your customers to come back, you better take good care of them and this page should be designed to do exactly this.

Blog:

Your customer will love you more if you have the time and resources to add a blog to your site. I will talk about blogs in much more details later. Blogs can contribute a lot to your success.

Podcast:

This is another good thing that you can add to your web site. Podcasts are another way to provide your customers with more target information. I will tell you more about podcasting later in the book.

Newsletter:

Newsletters are regularly published. It could be weekly or monthly. I recommend it to be monthly and loaded with valuable information and news about your products and activity. It should be available for download or can be sent by email to your registered customers. This can help you broaden your customer base, keep your customers loyal and increase your sale volume. This newsletter should have news about the company and new products, sales, discounts, promotions, good tips and entertaining or amusing content.

Chapter 5

Web Site Development

This chapter is devoted to the actual process of building and publishing your web site. When it comes to building your web site, you have two choices. It all depends on your level of expertise and how much resources you are willing to put into that project. If you do not have a lot of money to spend and you do not have a lot of experience building web sites from scratch, your hosting company can be a goldmine for you. Most of the hosting companies have the resources and the tools to help you build a good and professional web site that can work for you. The good news is that this can be done very quickly. Every hosting company has a software, usually called web site editor, that can build a web site either from scratch or using one of the hundreds of what they call web site templates that they have. You do not have to know any computer programming or HTML to do this. All you need to do is to have a look at the available templates, pick up the one that is close to your business idea, then try to customize it to fit your needs. What I mean by customizing your template is that if you feel you need more pages, you can add the necessary pages, if you feel there are some web pages that you do not need, you can delete the unnecessary web pages. You can also change the look and the layout and you can add more tools and elements to the design but there are limits to what you can do. Two important things you need to do before starting to build your web site this way. The first thing is that you need to learn everything about your hosting company's web site editor. It is only easy to use after you learn it. There is a short learning period you have to go through. Every company's web site editor is different and you have to get familiar with it first. Pay great attention to what it can do. Usually every hosting company has an information center that has tutorials about how to use their web site editor. The second thing is that before starting the actual building of your web site, prepare everything ahead, the content and the elements you going to add. Remember that everything should be in a digital form. One thing that you should start thinking about early in time is your company's logo. This takes time to think about, design and implement. All the web site text should be prepared in advance, including main page text, product description text, all about page text, contact information page text etc. Of course, you will include photos in your web site. All these photos should be ready. Pay great attention to the photos of the different products you will have. These photos should be plenty, of high quality, and show all the details. This will help your customers to make their decision whether to order from your web site. Your product photos are so important that you should invest some money on a high quality scanner to scan small tiny objects and high quality digital camera. You can also use some nonspecific photos to enhance your site. There are thousands of high quality photos on the Internet. You can download as many as you want for free. Just go to any search engine web site and search for free photos. If necessary, you can include animation element, audio and video elements in your web site, but try to prepare them in advance.

The biggest drawback to using host company's template is that there are limitations to what you can do especially when it comes to future expansion. There is a limitation to your ability to grow and expand the functionality of your web site in the future.

On the other hand, if you are interested in building a career as a web developer or you intend to build an extremely powerful and dynamic Ecommerce web site or you have deep pockets to pay for a web designer or web developer, you are better off building your web site from scratch using the powerful tools available in the market. I advise everyone especially young people to go this way because the Internet is not just a temporary phenomenon, the Internet is here to stay. I can tell you that it is a long course of learning but you have to do it. It is the future. You can use your expertise to build your own web sites and turn around and sell them. You can make a lot of money helping other people and businesses build professional web sites.

When it comes to web site development, the competition now is between the open source and Microsoft. I do not advocate using the open source model at all. You should ask yourself this question: " Who is behind the open source model ? ". It is mainly non reliable partners and individuals. That means if you build a web site using the open source and you run into some problems in the future, you are stuck and you could end up restarting all over again. Consulting fees for open source are very high and your chance of getting problems with open source is very high too. A lot of people think that the open source software is free. It is not. It will end up costing you more in terms of technical support, failures and limitations in functionality. The only good thing about open source software is that it is preventing a monopoly from Microsoft by providing some sort of competition and as you know, competition is good for the consumer.

I recommend for everyone to start learning the Microsoft ASP.NET framework. It is easy to learn and, using it, you can build the best web sites ever. Microsoft will be behind you in every step of the way and they are always improving their platform on a regular basis. So, if you want to build a career for yourself, you can do this by starting to learn the ASP.NET. Microsoft is taking web development seriously. There is no doubt in my mind that ASP.NET 3.5, the latest version, is the fastest, most efficient, most reliable and best supported way to create interactive web applications now. Using this platform and other development tools offered by Microsoft, some of them are free and some cost money, it is very easy to create web sites that look great and perform very well. The good news for the beginners is that the amount of code you need to write to implement quite complex things continues to decrease with each new version of ASP.NET. And with ASP.NET there is always more to come.

ASP.NET is relatively easy to learn compared to other programming languages and with ASP.NET there is always more to discover. There is a lot of support and free tutorials from Microsoft. Best of all, you can download all the software you need to help you in the learning process for free. After learning and starting to have confidence in yourself, then you can buy the commercial software and you are in business.

Chapter 6

ECOMMERCE

Ecommerce is the business of selling products, services etc over the Internet. A Ecommerce web site is nothing more than a regular web site plus three other components: A shopping cart, a payment processor and a merchant account. I will talk about each component in more detail later in the chapter.

Probably, you had an experience buying a product or a service over the Internet. What makes you prefer the online shopping is one of two things. The first is the fact that the price is too low compared to the retail store selling the same product. It is a bargain and you do not want to pass it out. The second is the fact that the item is rare and you can not find it somewhere else. These are the two main reasons people are buying things online. You should take this into consideration when building your web site. If you can not sell the products cheaper than retail stores, then forget it and move to something else.

In most cases, online shopping starts like this: A customer is looking for something. If he knows the web site, he will go directly to that web site. Otherwise, he will go directly to a search engine web site and search for what he is looking for. The search result will give him hundreds, probably thousands of possible sites. Most of the people will go only through the first ten or twenty names. That is why your site need to be highly ranked by different search engines. If the customer finds the item he is looking for, he will add this item to his shopping cart. When the customer is ready for a checkout, the shopping cart will place a request to the payment system. Ideally, the customer will click a button called " Place Order ". After clicking that button, the payment processor or gateway starts requesting credit authorization for the customer credit card. If the credit authorization is approved, your merchant account will request appropriate funds from the customer's credit card company then deposit the money into your bank account. In real world applications, all these three components merge into one system or solution that is usually offered by your hosting company or other companies you choose. A typical example of this is the PayPal payment system. It incorporates all of the three components into one solution. I will talk about PayPal later in the chapter.

Ecommerce Shopping Cart:

It is a software program that does some functions to help with the ordering process. When you click on an item to buy it, the shopping cart holds it for you till you finish your shopping process and ready to pay " empty the cart ". It is the same as a shopping cart in a physical store. When choosing a shopping cart, there are some considerations to take into your account. First, it should not cost too much, it will be much better if is free as a part of the package. Second, it should be compatible with other programs running your web site, especially the rest of the payment system. It should not be a big issue because most of them do, but you need to make sure by asking your hasting company technical support. Third and most important, it should be user friendly. It should give your customer a pleasant experience. Fourth, it should has the ability to discount coupons and other promotional discounts, add sales tax, if any, and compute and add shipping costs.

Payment Processors:

Sometimes they are called gateways. They represent some sort of a link between your shopping cart contents, your customer credit card and your merchant account. It comes to action only when the customer is ready to pay. This happens when he clicks a button called " BUY" or " ORDER ". After the shopping cart figure out the total amount, it sends an input to the gateway. The gateway, then, request customer credit card authorization for that amount of money and ask for that amount to be deposited into your merchant account.

Merchant Account:

This is the account you need to have with a credit card processing company or a commercial bank. It collects the money from your customer and deposits it into your account. It used to cost too much and you need to meet certain criteria to be able to open one but prices now are going way down thanks to the PayPal payment system.

Two great payment systems are PayPal, owned by eBay, and Google Checkout, owned by Google. These two are so successful that they deprive the banks from a good source of income that they used to get from businesses trying to open merchant accounts. These merchant accounts used to cost a lot of money to open and maintain, but thanks to the Internet, PayPal and Google Checkout, prices are coming down and practically anyone can easily open a merchant account. I will talk about both systems in much more details later in the book.

When talking about Ecommerce, a good payment system is only one aspect of a successful Ecommerce business. There are other things you need to consider to succeed in this field. You need to design your web site in a way that is appealing to your customers, depending on the products or services you are offering. For a successful Ecommerce web site, you need to adopt great marketing techniques. Marketing is a very big issue. For the purpose of this book, I am just giving you an idea about what an Ecommerce web site should have and look like. To be successful in Ecommerce, you need to get to the details. Read as much as you can about Ecommerce good practices. Learn from the experts in the field. Go to other commercial web sites and study the details especially what they do to attract more customers. There are thousands even millions of commercial web sites. All of them have one thing in common. They have a formula for success. They have adopted different strategies not just to stay in business but to make money. You do not need to invent anything. Just look at what these pioneers have done and try to do the same. If you can do something more to gain the competitive advantage, that will be even better. Try to live within your means. Spend what is only necessary to stay in business because you do not know what is going to happen. There is no one hundred percent guarantee that you will succeed but, at least, you will learn from your experience.

Chapter 7

WEB SITE OPTIMIZATION

You need to have a lot of visitors to your web site. This is the ultimate goal. Put it this way: No traffic, No business. To achieve your goal of web site optimization, there are things you need to do to make your web site usable.

The best way, on the long run, to get traffic to your web site is to have good content, something that people want all the time. The contents of your web site should be useful, updated on a timely manner and fill a need. Go check the big sites on the net and see what they are doing to attract more visitors. If you have a good content, the search engines will respect your web site and it will be ranked high and this way you will even get more visitors. The content of your web site should be relevant to your activity. If you are selling digital cameras, your content should be about photography. I will talk about good content later in the marketing chapter.

To attract more visitors to your web site you need to design it in a way that makes it that makes it easy to navigate and download fast. People who are surfing the net do not have the time to wait for your web site to download unless your web site is unique and there is no alternative to it. They will wait for seconds then they will go somewhere else. Your web site will not download fast if you have a lot of graphics or if you have a lot of visitors compared to your Internet connection speed. A very great technology, introduced by Microsoft, can make your web site download fast. It is called AJAX.

The first thing you need to do even before you publish your web site, is to list it with at least with the big search engines like Google, Yahoo, Microsoft, Ask.com etc. This is extremely important because it takes a lot time to get listed. It may take months before your web site appears in any search or get a good rank. Also, you need to do what they call search engine optimization either by yourself or with the help of a professional. I will talk about search engine optimization later in a separate chapter. You can list your web site for free by visiting each web site and submit some kind of a form.

For Google go to http://www.google.com/addURL.

For Yahoo go to http://www.yahoo.com/submit.

For Microsoft go to http://search.msn.com/docs/submit.aspx.

And so on.

One thing to remember is that even if you get a high ranking place with search engines, it will not do you any good if you do not have good content or something that people want.

If you are looking for fast exposure you have to spend money on advertising. There are all kinds of advertising. The most cost effective way of advertising is through Google AdWords. The best thing about it is that it is designed to fit all budgets and it produces immediate results. I will discuss all of this in the marketing chapter.

Chapter 8

SEARCH ENGINE OPTIMIZATION

Most people who are surfing the net are looking for something. What most people do when looking for something online is to go to a search engine and write few words then click a button. The result is that they get hundreds and in some cases, thousands of pages. Of course, they can't review all of these pages. Most of the people review only the first page which mounts to about twenty web sites. So, if you are not ranked in the first page, you are out of luck. You will have no chance of getting any of these free visitors.

There are hundreds of search engine web sites but only Google, Yahoo and Microsoft have a lion share. Google is way up at the top, followed by Yahoo then Microsoft comes third. The battle for searches is fierce because whoever controls it will the most of the online ads revenue. That is why Microsoft has recently teamed up with Yahoo to take on their rival, Google.

Search engine optimization is a process in which you do some modifications or positive changes to your web site. These modifications are supposed to give you high ranking among the top three search engines. Search engine optimization is a long ongoing process. Some companies which have deep pockets leave it to the experts. Even with these experts, unless you have a well designed web site with good content, there is a limit to what these experts can do. If you are on a budget, you can try to do this process by yourself. First, you need to know how search engines work. Most search engines, including Google, collect information about the millions of different web sites that make up the net using mostly three methods. The first method is by taking advantage of what is called user input. Everyone who creates and publishes a web site will go ahead and list it with as many search engines as he can. This listing process is a great source of free information for search engines. The second method is the fact that some search engines have developed some kind of software called spiders or crawlers. These crawlers go through the internet collecting all kinds of information about new and existing web sites. They are always on the look for any changes on the web. That is why they are very sensitive to blogs because blogs are updated on a regular basis. The third method is through collaboration and partnership with the World Directory of Web Sites. This is an Organization, called the Open Directory Project, that is made up of thousands of human volunteers all over the world. Their job is to web sites, review them and compile data manually about these web sites. These compiled data is collected in a big directory that is used by search engines to further tune up their job of searching. You can list your site in this directory for free. All you need to do is to visit their web site at http://www.DMOZ.org then ask for your site to be listed. The data and the information they collect is used by the main search engines like Google, Yahoo and Microsoft. After search engine collect that information, they do something called processing the data. They categorize, classify and rank that information in accordance with certain criteria. The number one criterion is, without doubt, content. A well designed web site with great content will naturally rise to the top without even any optimization. Another criterion that is used by many search engines to rank web sites is what is called good keywords. Usually these keywords you add at the top of your HTML code of your main home page.

A good way to know more about the subject of keyword, what they are and where to put them is to visit good high ranking web sites. On your web browser, there a tab called the view tab. Click that view tab and select source. This will give you the whole source code of that page. Look at the keywords that is inserted within the HTML code. After learning about keywords, do the same thing with your competitors' web sites. Write down what keywords are using. To get some more good keywords to include in your web site, go to that web site: http://www.goodkeywords.com. This web site can supply you with some good keywords. All you need to do is to write down the main idea of your web site and they suggest to you the good keywords that you should use. Write them down. Now you have two lists of keyword, the one from your competitors' web sites and that second list. Combine the two lists together into one list and use it in your web site. The last thing that you need to worry about is what is called metatags. These metatags includes the most searched keywords for your activity. Imagine yourself a customer looking for something that you are selling, what possible keywords he can use to search and get to your web site using that search. You need to include them in the title of each page of your web site. You can also include them in the site description and the site summary. Most hosting companies have the tools to automatically incorporate metatags into your web site. Otherwise, there are lots of free tools online that can help you create them and incorporate them in your web site. There are also free tutorials. All you need to do is to make a search on Metatags creation.

The area of search engine optimization is broad and there are lots of details beyond the scope of this book. If you want to do it yourself you should read some books about the subject so you can do it right.

Another way to increase the chance of your web site to be ranked high is to increase links to other relevant web sites. This is a powerful tool and is not hard to do. You can exchange links with other web sites. You can submit articles to other web sites and encourage them to link to your web site.

I do not recommend using a professional help when it comes to search engine optimization for two reasons. The first is that their service is quite expensive. The second is the nature of the search engine optimization process itself. Even if you achieve a high ranking, it may not last for too long, simply because everyone is fighting for the same goal and using the same tools and strategy. It is a very long ongoing process and it is not cost effective if you seek the help of a professional. The only way to stay at the top for a longer period is to have great content. I advocate that you do this by yourself on a regular basis. You need to apply the general principals of usability which include good content and good design, easy navigation, fast downloading etc.

Chapter 9

Internet Marketing

Marketing your site is a big subject. It is a full time job and you have to come up with a marketing strategy that can make your web site prevail. Your goal is to extend your reach and build more and more audience all the time. There are lots of techniques to spread the word about your web site, get more visitors and make some cash. Most of these techniques are free. They only eat up your time and energy. Others cost you cash. I will talk first about the free techniques.

Web Site Optimization:

We talked about this before. I explained to you how important it is to have a web site that is well designed, download fast and has a lot of good content. There is no substitute for this. Also, I talked about how important it is to do search engine optimization.

Email marketing:

Once you have a good site and you are confident that your visitors will have a good experience visiting your site, you can start the process of building up your email list. Building an email list and keeping it current is a very tricky job. Before starting building your email list, you need to remember that most people will not bother coming to your web site unless you have something free to offer. Think about what things you can offer for free that will not cost you a dime. Again grab a pen and a piece of paper, then go and visit other web sites. The purpose of this visit this time is clear; to find out what things they offer for free. Write down what each site is offering people to entice them to come. After that visit you will come with lots of ideas. Some web sites are offering free articles. Others are offering free e-books, free how to, free software downloads. Some web sites are offering free games, others are offering sweepstakes and so on. Think about what is good for your site. You can not, for example, be selling shoes and offering free technology articles to your customers. But if you are running a kids web site, you can offer them free games. Once you decide on the free offer, your next step is to offer them a free membership or free sign up. This second step requires even more free stuff. Usually your customer will ask himself that question: " Why do I sign up for this site? What do am I getting out of this? ". This is very critical to your success. You need to have an answer for this. Once they sign up you have their email and this way you can build your email list. You need to promise them that your email list is very confidential. Our policy is : " We do not sell or rent email lists. ". It is a very good idea to have a weekly newsletter that you can email it to them with attractive offers to buy from you. The worst thing you can do is to bombard them with emails on a daily basis. People do not like this at all and you will not be able to keep your list for too long.

Articles For Review:

Writing articles has become a popular way to attract more visitors to your site and build high quality audience, especially if these articles are of high value and contain specialized information. This is another powerful tool that can work in your favor. Your first step, if you want to use articles as a way of marketing for your site, is to ask yourself that question: " What articles can be appropriate to the subject of my web site ? ". If your web site is about cocking, then your articles should have something to do with food, cocking and healthy food. You can include articles about how to lose weight and so on. Sometimes, it happens that you do not have the writing skills to write articles. Do not drop the whole issue of your mind. You can ask for volunteers to write articles for you. Ask your audience to post articles in your web site. There are thousands of articles on the net that you can download and post in your web site. All are free and legal. Finally you can hire someone to do the writing for you. Go to http://www.RentAcoder.com. You will find lots of good writers for a very reasonable price. All you need to do is to explain them exactly what kinds of articles you want. Make sure they choose a very attractive title or heading to the article because this is what attracts people to read these article. Once you have these high quality articles ready, you can do two things with them. The first thing is to post them in your web site. The second thing is to submit them to as many web sites as you can, because these sites will put your name as the owner of the article and provide a link for your web site. This will increase the popularity of your web site. There are lots of web sites that can do this for you, saving you time and effort. Their activity is to publish articles for republication by other web sites. This is where you can find free articles for your site. To find them go to any search engine and search for " Article Directories ". The most well known of these sites are: http://www.GoArticles.Com and http://www.ArticleCity.Com. To increase your credibility and popularity, you need to submit more articles to these sites on a regular basis. Once all these sites link to your site you will get two benefits. You will get more visitors and build more audience. Your ranking will improve with different search engines.

Newsletters:

A newsletter can help you in two ways. First it can increase traffic to your site especially if it offers something useful and visitors will benefit from it. Second, it will help you build and maintain a viable email list. You can have a weekly or monthly newsletter that you post in your web site and email it to your email list.

Writing a newsletter is an art. If it is not good enough, you will be wasting your time. Think about it. How many newsletters we get in our email and we never even bother to look at. It is better to have a good monthly newsletter than to have a weekly one that nobody will look at. The best way to do it is to imagine yourself as a visitor to your site and design it accordingly.

Your Own Blog:

If you can add a blog to your site, that will be a great idea. Search engines love blogs because their contents are constantly updated. So having a blog will boast your hopes for a high ranking among different search engines. Also, having a blog will help you build your email list. Blogs are so important in helping you make money that I will discuss them in more details in a separate chapter.

Podcasting:

You can go fancy and add podcasting to your web site. Podcasting is nothing more than adding audio and video clips to your web site. That is the wave of the future and the widespread of broadband connection is helping that trend a lot. Should you like the idea of podcasting, there will be a separate chapter with a lot of details about podcasting.

Webinars:

Webinars are great new tools for online marketing. They are some sort of seminars or presentations online. These tools have a lot of future ahead of them and I will discuss them in a separate chapter.

Affiliate Programs:

Affiliate program are a great way to make money and grow bigger. There are two ways to use them. If you are selling a product or a service, you can have your own affiliate program and let other people join. You can also join affiliate programs of other web sites, helping them selling their products and make money this way. Affiliate programs can be a great source of income to those having web sites. I have a separate chapter in this book just for this subject.

Social Networking Sites:

Social networking sites have millions of visitors and millions of members. You need to have a presence and be active in all of them. Once you are there, you can promote your business. Your goal is to get some of these visitors to be your customers. Social networking sites are very important to any online business that I have a separate chapter for them in that book.

Video Sharing Sites:

Video sharing sites are very strong tools you can use to promote your site. You can create video clips that is designed to attract more visitors to your site and upload them for free in video sharing web sites like YouTube, http://www.youtube.com. Also you can upload them to Yahoo video at http://video.yahoo.com. The whole world can watch your video clips. You can even distribute them through Apple iTunes at http://www.apple.com/itunes. Video sharing web sites are great, you can make money of them even if you do not have a web site. I devoted one chapter for them.

Business Networking Sites:

Business networking sites represent another great way to promote your business. You need to be a member in each one of these sites. You can exchange information, get more visitors to your web site and gain more exposure. I devoted a whole chapter to this topic.

News Groups:

There are lots of news groups and chat rooms everywhere in the web. You need to be active but be careful not to waste your time. You need to figure out a target audience and try to reach them. Otherwise, it is a waste of time.

Free Classifieds:

A good example of free classifieds is Craig's list where you can post free ads. There are lots of places in the Internet where you can promote your web site for free and post ads. It does not cost you any money to do this. Go to any search engine and search for free classifieds.

Public Relations:

Your goal here is to reach the traditional media like TV, Radio and newspapers. Traditional media have reporters, editors, journalists and writers who are always looking for news, new technology, stories etc. If can convince them that you have something new, amusing, interesting or deserve to be mentioned, you win that free publicity.

There is a lot of talk about what is called a press release. A press release is nothing more than a short article that inform about your company and what they can offer to the public and why your offering is so unique that it deserves to be mentioned. The problem is that every day the media is bombarded with hundreds of press releases that no one has the time to look at. The trick is to develop some kind of relationship with those in charge. If you are a small guy with a normal web site, do not even bother. You need to come up with a strong new idea to be even considered. Some people even talk about TV talk shows, seminars and presentations. All of these are out your reach and you need to work very hard to be considered. You need to think about this as a last step. Do other steps first.

There are many other things you can do for free to promote your web site. You can also be creative and have your own techniques.

Now we discuss the techniques that will cost you money. Before you jump into anyone of these, you need to think a lot. You need to get your money worth. There are lots of ways to spend that money that is allocated for advertising. You can advertise your web site in traditional media like newspapers, TV, Radio etc. Though prices fall down, it is still not cost effective and you need lots of money. You can also use online advertising like putting banner ads in other web sites but it costs a lot and generally not very effective. You can also pay for premium placement in search engines. Most search engines have what is called Directories where you can be listed for a lot of fees. It is just expensive for any startup company. I found out that you can get a lot of your advertising dollar by using what is called Google AdWords. It is a very cost effective way to get traffic to your site. The best thing is that traffic is right on target, those who are interested in your product. Google have about 200 millions plus visitors each day. You can take advantage of this if you sign up for AdWords. You need to go to Google web site and read all the details about Google AdWords. A good thing is that you can only get what fits into your budget. If you have some money to spend on marketing, AdWords is the first thing you should set up. It will help you attract a lot of visitors and it will also help you build a great email list. Another great way to advertise is through the social networking sites. These networking sites have not been making any money, though they have millions of visitors every day. So, they started to figure a way to make money, and that has been online advertising. For example, Facebook.com which has millions of members has now its advertising program. Advertisers can choose pay-per-click ads which is similar to Google's auction ad program. Advertisers will bid on words and pay when someone clicks on their ads. Advertisers can also choose traditional ads that are based on impressions or the number of times an ad is presented. The good thing about advertising in Facebook.com is that your ads will go to a target audience and this way you will get your money worth.

Whatever appropriate media outlet you select to advertise, you need to focus on reaching a target audience in a cost effective manner. It does not pay you any good to reach just any audience. You need visitors who are interested in what you are offering. Reaching the wrong audience will not only cost you money but it will also consume a lot of bandwidth that you need for your loyal customers. Your goal is to spend the least amount of money to reach the largest number of your target audience. Sometimes you have to combine different media advertising, if your budget allows this. Since you have control over the contents of your ads, try to be creative to get the best response rate.

Chapter 10

Making Money with your Web Site

How can I make money with my web site? Probably you have heard this question hundreds of times, and you will hear it again and again. Most of the people are building web sites to make money. Few are those who build web sites for fun, personal reasons or to prove how good they are. Generally, there are four ways to make money of a web site:

Selling a product or service:

You can set up a web site to sell something physical like computers, shoes etc. You can also set up a web site to sell services, information, memberships, courses etc. This kind of web sites needs to have a shopping cart, a payment system and a merchant account. Your customer place the order, you collect the money. Generally, it is the most expensive way of making money online because of the high cost involved.

Advertising:

There is a lot of money to be made here. All you have to do is to build a web site that can attract a lot of audience. You need to have a lot of traffic, otherwise, you will not make a dime. How can you attract visitors? The answer is one word, Content. Good content is king on the Internet. Web sites that have a lot of good content, that are frequently updated, are search engines' good friends. They rank them high. They attract serious visitors. Most of these web sites make their money by signing up for Google AdSense program. Google has introduced a wonderful advertising program called Google AdSense. When you sign up for this program Google will place ads in your web site and pays you when visitors coming to your web site see the ad and click the ad to go to the advertiser's web site. It is called pay per click which means you get paid whether the advertiser makes a sale or not, you get paid per click. The amount you get paid depends on how much the advertiser is paying Google for his ad. Remember the more clicks you have, the more money you can make. You need to go to the Google site and check out this opportunity because it can be a good source of income to you. With this kind of web site you do not need to have a shopping cart, payment system or even a merchant account. This web site is easy to design, build and maintain. Your only problem is how to attract visitors.

Affiliate Programs:

This is another good source of income for people with web sites. Probably you came across a web site that is made of nothing but a lot of links to other web sites and a list of recommendations. These are links to affiliates. You do not have to build a fancy web site. I saw a lot of primitive web sites that are mainly designed to make money of affiliates. It is better, of course, to present a professional image by having a well designed web site with good content. This way you will have credibility and people will believe your recommendations. There are thousands of affiliate programs you can sign for and I will have a separate chapter on this topic.

A Web Site for Sale:

A lot of people just build a web site to sell it. They come up with a new idea targeting a specific big company like Microsoft, Google and others. Thousands of web sites have been sold so far and we see it every day. A good example, PayPal sold to eBay, YouTube sold to Google and so on. If you are creative, you have the technology and you have the good ideas, you can build up a web site and put it up for sale. If you come up with new ideas you can make millions of dollars. First, before you start, make a list of possible buyers. Go through the list and figure out what each of these companies is missing, or if your idea is going to add value to any of these companies. What is the possibility that your web site can be sold, for example, to Microsoft. If you do not have great ideas and you are just good at building web sites you can just use existing ideas and sell these web sites on eBay at a reasonable price. Offer some sort of technical support for a specific period of time. If you have a good domain for your web site, the price will go up.

These are the most ways people can make money of web sites. They are not separate. Actually, people use the four strategies together. A lot of people do not want to bother having a shopping cart, a payment system and a merchant account, so they just combine the last three strategies together and it can work for them real good.

Chapter 11

eBay; the King of the Jungle

There is no doubt in my mind that eBay has changed the way we do business. Now you can have your own business practically with no start up money. You do not even need to have a web site to do business on eBay. You do not even need to own a computer. You just go to the library and do your business there. The good thing is that the cost of doing business on eBay is so low that anyone can do it and can compete head to head with the big guys. It is a fact that eBay does all the marketing for you and bring the customers to your door steps. All you have to do is to convince them to buy from you. You do not have to spend a dime on advertising. So, when it comes to selling on eBay, big companies with deep pockets do not have any advantage over you.

Most people who are now eBay members started by selling used stuff around their houses, anything setting in home collecting dust or anything they do not need. It is like experimenting before they commit themselves and this is normal. At least, the risk will be minimal.

If you like to make some money on eBay, you need to sign up and join as soon as you can. It is very easy to become an eBay member. All you need is an email address and if you need to become a seller, you need to give them information about your checking account.

Everything is sold on eBay auction style. If you need to sell an item on eBay, you need to list that item first. To list your item for auction, you start with the title. It is very important to have an appealing and attractive title. Then you have to select a category. It is very important to list your item in the right category. Then you have the chance to describe your item. It is very important to provide your customers with a lot of details about your item. Do not over exaggerate. Say the truth. If the item is used, do not say it is new. There are lots of statements that can get you in trouble like almost new, hardly used, like new and so on. Try to be very cautious when using such statements. If your item has a problem, mention that problem. Do not say that it is working and ignore the problem it has. If you are not looking for trouble, just say the truth and nothing but the truth. EBay gives you the chance to provide a free picture of your item. Take advantage of this free offer. Pictures are a must on eBay. Then you need to price your item. Pricing your item is a very tricky business. If your price is too high, no one will buy from you. If your price is too low, you will end up losing money. When it comes to pricing, everyone has his own strategy and you will learn by experimenting till you develop your own strategy. Then you need to select the period of your auction. Typically, you can select 1, 3, 5, 7, or 10 days. If you choose 10 days, you will pay extra which is not good. I usually stick with the 7 days period. Then you have to specify a shipping method and how much you are going to charge for shipping. Do not overcharge your customers for shipping. Some people get really mad about this. If you are planning to charge more for shipping, mention why you are doing this. Some sellers argue that shipping is more than just the cost of postage. It is handing, packing, shipping materials in addition to a trip to the post office. It is time consuming and time is money. Other sellers say, " We charge more for shipping because we price our items very low; we do not have to pay high fees to eBay. Then you have to specify the method of payment which mostly is PayPal.

If you want to succeed in eBay, you have to have excellent customer service. You need to answer questions and inquiries as soon as you get them. Do not ignore or delay. Answer even rude questions. People get very angry if you ignore them or you do not answer them fast. It happened to me personally. Check your email daily. Present your auction with complete information. You should be honest in your description. Do not hide anything. If you try to hide something, sooner or later, the buyer will know about it you can get your item back. The buyer will not only ask for his money back, but he will give you a negative feedback. If you get too negative people will not even look at your auctions and eBay may cancel your membership and you will never be able to get back to eBay. Quick shipping is a must. After shipping the item to the winner of your auction, immediately, email him telling that the item is on the way and thank him for his purchase. Also, mention that in case of any problem with the item to contact you personally.

Pay great attention to eBay fees. It can eat up your profit. You can even lose money. The problem with eBay is that eBay charges you money to list your item. You lose that money whether your item sells or not. There is no guarantee that your item is going to sell. I found out that almost every month or every other month, eBay offers a one day of free listing. You should take advantage of this and get ready with all the items you are willing to list. You can list as many items as you can during that day free of charge. If some of your items do not sell, you do not lose any money. Few days age eBay announced that each seller can list up to five items for free every month. That is good news. I usually reserve this for the items that cost a lot of money to list.

Another cost is that eBay offers other fancy features e.g. extra pictures, subtitles etc., to make your item sell faster and get you more for your item. Another way to get more of your money is what is called featured listing. All of this costs you more money and extra fees. Do not go for it. Try to list with the minimal cost.

Pricing your item, as I said before, is very tricky. A big problem with eBay is that most of its members are bargain hunters, looking for something for nothing. So, if you price your item too high, your chance of getting a bid is zero. You need to price your item way below the market value. To make money with this kind of audience, you need to get your items very cheap, from garage sales, closeouts etc. Generally, people consider buying from an eBay auction a risky business but they are willing to take that risk if they get something in return. That something can be lower price or a bargain. Your best strategy is to find out how much a similar item was sold before on eBay and price your item accordingly.

When listing your item you have the option to state a reserve price. This means that you do not have to sell your item unless the price is equal to or more than the reserve price. I am against setting a reserve price for two reasons. First it will cost you more money which is not good. Second, I found out that the majority of eBay customers, including me, do not even bother to bid on items that have a reserve price.

There is no problem finding merchandise to sell on eBay as long as you stick to the rule, pennies on the dollar. A lot of eBay professionals recommend that you buy from wholesalers and manufacturers. I do not recommend this for two reasons. First, by the time you pay all the fees like eBay fees, PayPal fees etc., you will end up making no money because as I told you, to succeed in eBay, you have to offer items far below their market value. The second problem is that once you start dealing with wholesalers you need a sales tax license because wholesalers must collect sales tax on everything they sell to the general public unless you have a sales tax license. Then you are supposed to collect taxes from your customers which will make your items look more expensive and you have to lower your prices even more and this can eat up your profit.

Other eBay professionals recommend that you deal with what is called drop-shippers. It is simply you sell the product then you notify the drop-shipper to ship the product to the buyer. I do not recommend it at all for anyone who is doing business on eBay. First, they charge you higher prices which in turn can affect your profitability. Second, you do not guarantee the quality of the product. Third, you do not have any control over the shipping process. Sometimes the drop-shipper is out of that item you are listing and someone already put a bid on it. If this happens, you will be in big trouble. So, avoid this kind of deal. Unless you have the item or the product in your garage or basement, do not list it.

The only way to make profit on eBay is to have the ability to buy item for pennies on the dollar. Think about it. If you can find a way to buy items very cheap compared to their actual retail prices, you will be able to make money on eBay. Garage sales are good places, out of business sales, antique deals and so on.

I would like to talk about the feedback in eBay. It is an eBay system that lets the buyer evaluate you and this system can greatly affect your eBay business. If you have lots of negatives, no one will even think of bidding on your items. If your feedback score fall below fifty percent, eBay will cancel your membership and you will not be able to use eBay anymore. You need to keep an excellent feedback. The way to do this is through excellent customer service. Always tell your customers to contact you first, should they have any problem with the whole transaction. Try to solve their problems even if you have to lose some money. Most of the customers are fair and honest. Very few people are nuts and one way or another you have to deal with one of them. So your strategy is to protect your business.

Part of a good customer service is to offer your customers as many different ways to pay for their items as you can. Usually the most popular way of payment is PayPal. You need to sign up for PayPal as soon as you can. If you do not offer PayPal as a payment method, no one will bother looking at your items unless they are unique. PayPal is so important that I will discuss it in much more details in a separate chapter.

Offer your customers the option to pay by check but make it clear that you will not ship the item unless the check is cleared. Offer them the option to pay by money order. If you get paid by check or money order, you save the PayPal fees.

One more thing I would like to mention about eBay. If you can not make money selling on eBay, you can still join the millions of bargain hunters on eBay. You can save a lot of money by buying what you need from eBay. That is what I do. I buy software, hardware, electronics and other things from eBay and other Internet sites.

Finally, a lot of people ask me that question, " I am doing very good on eBay. Should I quit my regular job and do eBay full time? ". My answer is a big no. The reason is very simple. On eBay, you do not own or control your destiny. You are under the mercy of your customers. Not all the customers are nice and forgiving. No matter how good and careful you are, mistakes can unintentionally be done. Adding to this, very few customers are nuts by nature. From time to time you can be stuck with someone who is nuts and wants something for nothing. He can cause you a lot of trouble and once you are out of eBay you lose your lucrative income. So, my advice to you is that if you do not have the time to do the work, hire your kids, your spouse or someone else who can work for a minimum wage but do not quit your job. Do not you know that eBay was actually designed to be a second income!

Chapter 12

Other Internet Auctions

If you think that eBay is the only Internet auction, you are wrong. There are lots of Internet auctions over there. Some of them have started long time ago, trying to take over eBay, but so far they have been unsuccessful. Others have started recently. Go to any search engine and search for Internet auctions, you will get a very long list. I will mention some of these auctions here just to give you an idea and because I have tried them. If you are serious about making money online, you need to visit each one of them. May be you can find a unique chance somewhere.

PROPERTYROOM.COM:

It is one of the largest collections of unique items and bargains on the Internet. It is a collection of stolen, seized, recovered, unclaimed and surplus items for law enforcement agencies from coast to coast. All these items can be found everyday on http://www.propertyroom.com. The best way to get started is to browse or search through the PropertyRoom.com auction categories and listings to see what kinds of items are offered for auction. Categories along the left side will guide you, or you can search for specific items too. If you see something you would like to bid on, you must first register. Browsing, searching and registration are all free. You only pay for items you purchase or win at auction. PropertyRoom.com inventory is never the same, so always check back to see what is new. I use this site to buy cheap items that I need or for resale on eBay. You can do the same thing; buy cheap from PropertyRoom.com and sell for profit on eBay. This can be a good strategy. Registration on PropertyRoom.com is free. There is no monthly membership fee and there is no obligation to maintain your membership. Once you have submitted your registration you will receive a confirmation email message and you will have instant access to PropertRoom.com products.

Http://www.PropertyRoom.Com is a unique e-commerce market place. It features goods seized and found by law enforcement agencies. Additionally, it offers items from trusted merchants in a variety of hot e-commerce categories including electronics, collectibles, jewelry, sports equipments and much more.

PropertyRoom.com claims that it has over 600,000 registered bidders, 15,000 to 20,000 unique visitors daily and 500 auctions closed daily. If you need to apply to be a seller on this site, you need to meet high performance expectations and have a proven track record of excellence. For the purpose of this book, most people do not fit into that criterion. So my advice to you is to use this site to pick up bargains as I do and sell them on eBay for a profit.

Http://www.DellAuction.Com:

If you are a computer guy and like to deal with computers, this web site is a good chance for you to buy cheap, almost new desktops and laptops and turn around to sell them on eBay or somewhere else. The best idea is to sell them locally so your customers do not have to pay for the shipping. To bid and buy from this site, you must be a registered bidder. Getting registered is simple, fast and absolutely free. Once you are a registered user, you can enjoy bidding and buying. To register, just click on " Register " at the top of the Dellauction's home page. Create your Dellauction user ID and Password. Then enter your contact information, your primary shipping address information as requested. Your information will be maintained secure with DFS. Dell auction does not require credit card information during the registration process. However, when you place a bid, you will be required to provide credit card information with a valid US billing address issued by a US Financial Institution. The registered billing address must match the billing address on the card. If you are the winning bidder, the credit card that you have entered will be charged the total amount of the order. Dell auction is committed to making your bidding and buying experience safe and secure. I always recommend buyers to take the time to know as much as possible about the item before bidding or buying. If you are interested in an item, review carefully the details of that item or product. In an auction, the highest bidder is the winner of the item. If you have spotted an item you would like to place a bid on, you can do this quickly and easily. There are lots of good things about Dell auction. Their web site is more than great. Their customer service is excellent. Their merchandise is of high quality. The only bad thing about Dell auction is the way it is designed. It is designed to bring more money to the site. The duration of the auction is automatically extended for an additional ten minutes whenever a bid is placed right before the end of the auction. The auction will close once all bidding activity has stopped for a period of ten minutes. This is called popcorn bidding. They claim that they want to give the chance to everybody to bid, but the fact is that the price of the item will be pushed way up especially if there is a competition. My advice to you is to bid on items that have received no bids which means there is no competition. I found out that the competition is very tough for laptops but when it comes to desktops, there is very few competition. Of course, when it comes to Dell auction, you can only buy, you are not allowed to sell anything on that site.

These are two good examples of other Internet auctions. There are many other Internet auctions that let you not only to buy but also to list and sell your item. Most of these auctions offer free listing. So, it does not hurt to experiment with them and list as many item as you can. It is a way to check them out. They only charge you if your item sells.

The only bad thing about these auctions is that they do not have a broad customer base like eBay. Being unpopular may prove to be a good thing for you. You can buy cheap from these auctions and sell high on eBay. But a word of caution, you need to be careful buying from these sites. There are lots of frauds and scams compared to eBay.

When it comes to Internet auctions, so far, I haven't seen a real competitor to eBay.

Chapter 13

Better Than an Auction

Http://www.ioffer.com:

This is a great web site; better than an auction. It is unique and I used it a lot. The good thing about this site is that, unlike eBay, they do not charge you any listing fees. The bad thing is that it is still far behind eBay in terms of popularity.

Ioffer is free for buyers. Sellers only pay a small fee after an item is sold. As with other web sites, you need to register to be a member before you can use the web site. You will need to create a user ID and a password. Also, you will need a valid address and an email. You can register without using a credit card, however, in order to list items for sale, you need to do one of the following:

Place a credit card on file (full seller account to list in all categories).

Make a payment with PayPal of at least $20.00 (funds will be deducted from your account balance).

Send in a pre-payment of at least $20.00 (for seller fees incurred in the future).

After you become a member you will have what is called myioffer. Myioffer is the gateway to all of your account activities and transactions. From here you access to the following: Messages, Buying activity, Swapping activity, Selling activity, Member profile, Account information and Ratings.

Selling on ioffer is fast and easy and does not cost anything until your item sells. Simply, list your item and state your asking price. Then you let the buyer makes his offer. If you do not like his offer, you can make another counteroffer. It is a matter of negotiating till you agree upon something and the item is sold. If you do not agree, you or the buyer can stop the process any time. You can list a single item at a time or you can list 10 items or you can list 10,000 items in just a few clicks of your mouse. Ioffer, also have a tool called Mr. Grabber. Mr. Grabber is a powerful tool that allow you to bring over your feedback rating from eBay, Overstock and sell.com.

Benefits of selling on ioffer:

No listing fees. It is free to list. You only pay a reasonable fee when your item sells. Ioffer is in the business of encouraging sellers to list more. They have the least fees if you take a look at their fee comparison chart.

Free ioffer Store. List two or more items and get customizable store with integrated shopping cart. Ioffer has added dozens of new features to the stores, making it easier than ever to get your own personalized store up and running.

Ioffer claims that at anytime they have at least 28 million items for sale from 165 countries. Ioffer is an online community that allows you to sell and trade just like you would in real life by negotiating, better than an auction! Items listings will never expire until they are sold. As long as you are active (login at least once every 30 days) your item listings will remain live and searchable. Ioffer will send two notices before ending your items after 30 days of inactivity. Pictures uploads are free, unlike eBay which allows you to upload only one free picture, you need to upload more, you pay. So with ioffer you can enhance your item listings by adding enough free pictures to let buyer gain a good visual and understanding of your items.

It comes sometimes when you have a Nonpaying buyer or NPB. In this case, you can apply for NPB credit. You are eligible to file a Nonpaying Buyer and receive a refund of your final value fee if the buyer has not paid for the item, it is more than 21 days and less than 45 days after the completed transaction and you have sent at least two invoices to the buyer.

As with eBay, when you list items, your asking price should be far below the retail value. When customers submit an offer for you which is usually lower than your asking price you can accept or reject this offer. When you get an offer, think about it. If it reasonable and you think you are going to make some profit, you can accept it, otherwise, you are free to reject that offer. The risk of using that web site as a seller is very low, you can not lose any money. But if you are a buyer, you need to be very careful. There are scams over there especially if you are buying from somebody overseas.

Of course, you do not need to have a web site to make money with this web site. I encourage you to check it out. You will not lose anything.

Chapter 14

Cash For Used Books

Http://www.half.Com:

This is the one that I like most. You can make a couple hundred dollars a month for practically doing nothing. If you take it seriously, you can make much more. I found this opportunity by chance. I used to have a lot of books. I have been collecting books for years. First I joined book clubs. Book clubs work this way. First they drag your feet by giving you some free books if you become a member. Then after becoming a member, they send you a catalog of featured and new books. You browse the catalog and order whatever books you like. I could not resist buying the books I like. I kept buying and buying, though I did not have any time to read most of these books. My house was filled up with books so I canceled my membership with these clubs but I still have the appetite to buy more books. Every time I go to a garage sale or a church sale, the first thing I do is to visit the book section where I pick up few good titles. I am interested in business books, how to books, electronics and computer books. My house was filled up with books and I was running out of space and my wife was running out of patience. I felt some guilt about all these books setting around collecting all this dust and I do not have the time to read them. I usually go to garage sales with my wife. When I pick up a book, she does not say anything but I can see the dirty looks in her eyes. One day we got into that argument and I decided to stop buying any kind of books and started thinking of a way to get rid of them. I did not want to list them on eBay because eBay charges you money whether your books sell or not. One lucky day I was reading a magazine and there was an article about ways to make some extra money. A woman was telling her story about how she sold her used books on the Internet and made an easy $150.00. That web site is: http://www.half.com. I wrote down the name of that web site and I decided to check it out. The first thing I did was to collect all the information about it. To become a seller, you have to become a member of the half.com web site. Becoming a half.com user is easy. You will be asked to choose a user name and a password and to supply your real name, mailing address and an email address. Once you have agreed to the user agreement, click "continue" and you are signed up. It is that simple. At half.com, like all Internet sites, the member is fully responsible for choosing and maintaining control over his own password. At this time of writing this book, only persons residing within the fifty United States can buy or sell on half.com. If you have already become a member and want to sell on half.com, just follow the simple steps below:

1. Click the My Account link at the top of the page to login to your account.
2. Click the " Start Selling Now " link located on the " Selling " box on the left side of the page.
3. Enter your credit card and contact information and click next.
4. Enter in your direct deposit information in order to receive payments.
5. Choose the shipping methods you will support. You have to support Media Mail by default, but you can also opt to offer Expedited Mail to buyers. Click " Register " and you are done.

Half.com use your credit card information and telephone number to verify your identity and as another way to protect other members from fraud. Using the credit card processing network, half.com will verify that the name and billing address you entered match the name and billing address on the credit card.

You are not charged anything to register or list items for sale at half.com. As a seller, half.com only offer payment by direct deposit (ACH) to your personal checking account. The balance on your accumulated sales is calculated on the 15th and the last day of each month. Your payment will be deposited to your personal checking account approximately 7 business days after the end of the selling period. Savings accounts are not supported for direct deposit. When half.com is preparing to deposit monies in your checking account, they will send you an email letting you to know what date to expect the money. You need to sign up for direct deposit.

To list an item in books, music, movies or games, just follow these steps:

1. Click " Sell your Stuff " at the top of any page.
2. Find the UPC or ISBN number of the item you want to sell. Typically, the UPC or ISBN is found above or below the barcode on the item. Books usually have ISBN number. For all items other than books, enter the UPC and not the ISBN. Many movies, CDs and video games have ISBNs. You should ignore these.

3. Type the UPC or ISBN number in the entry box and click continue. Select a quality rating for the item and enter any comments about the item e.g. cover torn, stain on the back etc. Click on the continue button.
4. Next, select a price for the item. Half.com will recommend a price based on the quality of the item. You can set any price you want for your item. However, it is important to remember that the lower the price, the more likely it is to sell. Add a quantity and then click the " List Item " button and you are in business.

Once you list an item, half.com provides the cover art, review and product information from its extensive database. So, to list your items you simply enter the item's UPC or ISBN number and half.com takes care of the rest; piece of cake. You can also list your items through the AddItem API. Note that the minimum price you can list an item for is $00.75. The suggested selling price, which helps you price your product competitively, is calculated as a percentage of the best online retail price for a new copy of the item and depends on the quality of the item. Once you list an item on half.com the item will remain listed on the site either until it is sold or until you remove it from your inventory. There are no time limits on items listed. For this reason it is very important to manage your inventory carefully. If you sell an item outside of half.com or if an item gets damaged, you will want to be sure to remove the item from your inventory before someone purchases it. You can delete, edit or suspend any items you have currently listed.

Correctly assessing and representing the quality of an item is extremely important. Half.com buyers will be making purchase decisions based on quality ratings. After the sale, they will be rating their experience with each seller based in part on the accuracy of the quality ratings.

Half.com has shops. A half.com shop is a place on the site where buyers can come to see all the inventory offered by a particular seller. They will be also able to view important statistics about the seller. As a seller you automatically receive a half.com shop for free. Anytime a half.com member clicks on your seller name, he will be taken to your half.com shop. Here they will be able to browse your full inventory by drilling down into any categories that you have inventory in. Most importantly, these buyers will be able to buy an item directly from your store without seeing it offered from other sellers. One of the features that has been created along with half.com shops is the ability for any half.com member is the ability to maintain a " Favorite Sellers " list. A member can put any seller on his favorite list which will give him a place to go to buy from sellers who they have had a good experience with. When you provide great service, half.com will encourage you by asking your buyers to put you in their favorite sellers list and come back and check your inventory regularly.

When half.com created the new shops feature, they made even cheaper for buyers to find great values on half.com. Now when they buy more than one item from the same seller, shipping on subsequent items will be much cheaper. This additional shipping discount is being absorbed by half.com in an effort to encourage buyers to purchase more items from great sellers.

You can market your half.com shop in a variety of ways. You can tell customers, friends and family to visit your shop at your very own URL: http://shop.half.eBay.com/your-sell-name. You can also print package inserts for your buyers with your shop URL and ask them to place you on their favorite sellers list. Finally, you need to be creative.

Filling An Order:

The most important thing a seller can do is properly packaging and shipping orders. Good packaging and correct shipping methods help contribute to a good feedback rating and repeat sales. You will get an email from half.com for every sale you make. When you receive this email you have 72 hours, excluding weekends and holidays, to ship the item. A good idea is to use the site to print your shipping labels.

When you sell on half.com, you will receive a shipping credit or reimbursement to help cover the costs of shipping. The amount of the reimbursement depends on the type of product sold. The shipping allowance that half.com provides is sufficient to cover the cost of the vast majority of items that are sold at half.com. However, this allowance, may not be enough to cover the cost of shipping heavy books. In these case, you may want to adjust the price you set for the item to make up for any difference between what the US Postal service charges to ship the item and the shipping reimbursement. It is very important to have all your shipping insured or have a tracking to protect you as a seller from loss.

I hope that information is enough to get you started. Still if you need more information to start selling you can get back to that web site. Now back to my story. I found out that you can list as much used books as you can without costing you a dime. Best of all, when you sell a book, they collect the money for you and deposit it directly into your account which is a great deal. I signed up immediately and I listed all my books and CDs. Money started coming in. All I have to do is to ship the sold item by the USPS to the buyer's address. When I found out how easy it is to make money that way and started to run out of books, I tried to figure out a way to get more inventory. How I can get these books and CDs cheap was the question that was always in my mind all the time. I made a plan for myself. At any time I should have a list of more than 1000 of items. Also, from my experience, I found out that the books that sell fast on this web site are text books in general, electronics books. It does not mean that other books are not selling but these books are in high demand even if they are old editions. They sell fast and bring you more money. I found a way to get these books for pennies on the dollar. I go to church sales in my area where they offer what is called a bag sale. You fill up a bag with all kinds of stuff and you only pay 2 or 3 dollars each bag. I fill up my bags with the best books and CDs that I can put my hands on and I am in business. Another good source of cheap books is consignment stores. Also public libraries, web sites that offer free stuff like Craig's list and others. You need to figure a way to get these books for free or at least very cheap. If you going to pay money for a book, even a dollar, make sure you can use it if it does not sell.

Another way to use this site is to buy what you need at a very deep discount. On this web site, you can buy book, including audio books, Music CDs and Movies, Games and game systems and even gift certificates. There are several ways to find an item at half.com. The search bar on the Home Page lets you search for an item in the entire inventory. Click a category tab (books, music, movies, games or game systems) then do a more specific search by Title, Actor, Director, UPC, ISBN or Author. You can ask the seller a question about the item before buying. However, it is optional for sellers to respond to pre-purchase questions. If you are looking for an item and you can not find it on half.com inventory, you have two fantastic options:

First, you can add it to your Wish List. The Wish List allows you to specify the price and quality rating for the item you are looking for. An email will be sent to you as soon as the item becomes available. You can add an item to your Wish List by using the Wish List Link at the top of every item detail page.

Second, you can search an item on eBay, the world's online marketplace. As a half.com member, you are automatically registered with eBay, which means you can practically trade anything with practically anyone on earth. Since eBay bought half.com, your half.com member name and password are the same on eBay.

You can create a Favorite Sellers list. This list, which is stored in your account area, allows you to keep track of the sellers you prefer to deal with. There are many ways to do this but we want to keep it short.

Once you find your item click on it to get specific seller, pricing and quality information. When you are ready to buy, click the " BUY " button next to the specific item you want to put in your shopping cart. All purchases at half.com must be made with a valid credit card. At this time there are no plans to incorporate PayPal into the half.com site.

Chapter 15

Sell on PriceGrabber

Selling on this site is mainly based on price. If you can beat the other guys when it comes to price you win. You can also buy what you need at a reasonable price.

Http://www.PriceGrabber.Com is a shopping comparison web site. They do not sell any of the products on the site. They provide the customers with a list of vendors who carry the product and put them in order by price. Prior to selling on PriceGrabber.com you will need to sign up for an account. You will be asked for basic information including a valid credit card issued by a US Bank. You won't be able to start selling on PriceGrabber.com until you confirm your email address by following the instructions that the site will send to your email account during the sign up process. This setup is very easy to follow and it just ensures that the site and the buyers ordering from you will have your correct email address and other relevant information. You won't able to sell using PriceGrabber.com unless you are equipped to accept online payments.

There are two types of sellers on PriceGrabber.com: Storefronts and Merchants. PG Storefronts is a service designed to help sellers list and sell merchandise without the need to have their own web sites. This service can also help sellers who would rather pay commission only if their merchandise sells rather than a cost per click approach to send traffic to their own web sites.

Levels of Accounts:

1. Basic Member Account: Username plus password plus basic information.
2. Confirmed: Basic account plus confirmed email address.
3. Silver: Confirmed plus U.S. verified credit card.
4. Gold: Silver plus PayPal verified account.
5. Platinum: Gold plus approved application to increase trading limits.

Selling On PG Storefronts:

There are lots of benefits to selling on PG Storefronts. You can enhance your business and earn extra cash. Also, selling on PG Storefronts is fun, easy and fast. Members can list up to 50 products with no listing fee. You do need a web site to sell on PG.com. You can manage your listings very easily using the " Your Account " page. You can reach out to more than 26 millions unique visitors every month. You can list multiple products in bulk.

Requirements:

You may only use PG Storefronts to list and sell any item that is already included among the hundreds of thousands of items posted on PG.com. You will need a PG account to use PG Storefronts. Additionally, you will need to add a credit card to your PG account and confirm your email account. You won't be able to sell using the PG Storefronts unless you can receive payments through one of the accepted methods.

Fees:

The first 50 products may be listed for no listing fee. Products listed over the initial 50 products will be subject to a $0.10 USD per product per calendar month listing fee. Additionally, sellers shall pay a base commission rate ($1.50 plus 6.75% of the purchase price) after a product is sold.

Listing an Item:

When you find a product you want to sell on PG.Com, click on the " Sell Yours Here " link and the system will guide you through each step of the process. You will decide on a sales price, pick from a range of shipping options and select how to collect payment. Once you have a sale, PG will send you an email with details about this transaction. You can also check your activity by logging into your PG account.

If you can not find your product already listed on PG, your product can be considered to be manually added. Since PG has already listed millions of products, the web site typically add only those items that they feel would be mostly in demand by users. You can send an email request with the product name, model number, and manufacturer's link to info@pricegrabber.com and PG will get the process started.

Managing Your Sales:

After each sale or transaction, PG will send you an email with all the relevant information for that transaction. Using your account you can retrieve recent sales, contact buyers, add tracking numbers to inventory and manage customers' questions. You can also monitor reviews from buyers and see ratings from your customers.

Feedback:

One of the most important factors to drive sales is the reputation of the seller. PG recommends that you rate the buyer and request a rating from them in return.

Listing Multiple Products In Bulk:

If you have multiple items and you do not want to add them one by one, you can use the Bulk Import Grabber. It can save you time when adding and updating your listings using excel or your own CVS (Comma Separated Values) files.

PG recommends that if you have multiple items to list, it may be more efficient for you to list them using the Bulk Import Grabber. It is a feature that allows PG Storefronts sellers to update their inventory from a CSV file. Creating a CSV file is easy. Most of the popular spreadsheet applications, such as Microsoft Excel, allow you to save a file as a CSV file. CSV stands for Comma Separated Value, which basically means that your file will be saved as a text that has commas to delimit the columns of the original spreadsheet file.

Accepting Payments:

There are three basic ways of collecting payments when selling on PG Storefronts: PayPal, Credit cards and Google Checkout. It is very simple to link your verified PayPal account to your PG Storefront. Buyers will be forwarded to the PayPal web site at the end of the transaction and will complete their payments on PayPal.com's secure pages. PG receives payment updates from PayPal and keeps you updated on the status of the transactions. If you accept credit card payments already, you are most likely working with a credit card processor such as Paymentech, Card Services International, Nova or First Data Merchant Services.

Since credit card transactional information is very sensitive, you can not link your PG Storefronts directly to your credit card processor. You will need to use the services of companies known as Gateways. The main function of the gateways is to securely pass credit card information between your web site (in this case your PG storefronts account) and your credit card processor. There are few companies that offer the gateway service. PG supports the most important ones, which are the following: Authorize.net, Link Point, Verisign, ViaKLIX. If you already have an account with one of the above mentioned gateways, you will be able to link your PG Storefronts account to your gateway. If you do not have an account with a gateway, PG recommends that you first find out if your credit card processor is working with any of the gateways supported by PG. If this is the case, select the gateway that may be best for you and open an account with them.

Using Google Checkout is very straightforward. Buyers will be forwarded to the Google Checkout web site at the end of the transaction and will complete their payment on Google's secure pages. PG receives payment updates from Google and keeps you updated on the status of the transaction.

Sales Tax:

It is the seller's responsibility to determine the applicability of any sales tax. PG only requires that you agree not to charge more than the legal tax rate for your transaction.

A final advice for sellers is to include in your listing, as much detailed information as possible about your product as well as thorough description and competitive price. PG shows you the average price and also the highest price listed on PG, so you can price your merchandise accordingly. Sellers must also list the condition of each item they sell. There is a system scale starting with " New " and going to " Not Working ". A great way to illustrate the condition of your item is to add your own image of the item to your listing.

For the security of the PG members, new sellers can only sell a limited amount of dollars per month. If you expect to deal in higher priced merchandise or in larger sales volumes, you can contact PG at info@Pricegrabber.com so that they can review your account and determine if your account may be eligible for increased selling limits.

Buying From http://www.PriceGrabber.Com:

In order to make a purchase, you need to click on the " Shop " button on any product page next to the name of the retailer you want to buy from. If you know exactly what you are looking for, you can enter the manufacturer part number or keywords into the search box to go directly to the product. Select a product channel from the drop down menu to narrow your search results or leave it on " All products " to make your search broader. Detailed product specifications can be viewed for most products on PriceGrabber.com. Simply click the " product Details " tab on any product page to view this information.

On PG, there are two types of sellers: Storefronts and Merchants. To easily distinguish between the two, locate the product's page and listed below each seller's name is a title. From here it is pretty straightforward. If the title says " Storefronts ", it is a Storefront seller. However, if it says " Merchant Info " , then this is a PG Merchant seller.

Buying From a Storefront Seller:

Simply click the " Shop " button to visit the storefront for the seller. Once at the seller's Storefront, if you agree with the product and transaction details you can select the form of payment and the shipping method if the seller has provided various options. After selecting form of payment and shipping, click on the " BUY" button to continue. You will need to have a silver PG account in order to do this. If you do not already have one, you will be asked to create one at this point. Once you are logged into your PG account, you can complete the transaction. The listing for this item will be removed from PG and the Storefronts seller will be alerted that one of the items has been sold. PG will email your information about the total amount due as well as where to send your payment. Remember that all payments must be sent directly to the Storefronts seller, not to PriceGrabber.Com. The seller will ship your product after receiving payment. Under no circumstances should a buyer send cash to a seller to pay for a transaction.

Buying From a PG Merchant:

Once you have selected a PG Merchant from the listing on the product page, click the " Shop " button next to the merchant's name to go to their web site where you can place an order. You will need to create an account with the merchant even if you already have a PG account. The merchants are all separate companies from PriceGrabber.com.

Using PG services to make your purchases is absolutely free. As a Storefront buyer in good standing, you are protected up to $500.00 if the item is not received or if the sellers misrepresent their products.

<u>Final thoughts:</u>

I usually use PriceGrabber.com to sell some items and make some extra cash. Before listing any item I make sure that I am offering the lowest price. This is what you need to do. People will only buy from you if you have the lowest price. Again, you need to figure a way to get your item far below their retail value. If you can not do this, you will not be able to make any money.

Chapter 16

Selling Digital Information

Digital information is all kinds of information that can be downloaded, sent digitally to the customers or viewed over your web site. You do not have to own a web site to sell digital information. You need to know that more than 90% of those surfing the net are looking for information. That tells you there is a big market for such a product. But there are two common problems regarding selling information products online. The first problem is that we are living in the information age. There is not just an overload of information but an actual explosion. It will take you hours to look for a specific kind of information. People are confused, if you do not know where to look, you are going nowhere. The second problem has to deal with the kind of market we having right now on the Internet concerning such products. If you go and just have a look on eBay, for example, look at the category of digital information. You will find all kinds of stuff. Everyone is trying to sell everything and anything. There is a lot of junk over there for sale and the customers are confused. They do not know the good from the bad. There is a lot of mistrust. You will not be able to succeed in that field unless you have the right product, the right audience and the right marketing strategy. You need to build up trust and this will take a lot of time, effort and patience.

There are lots of good things about dealing with digital information. If you do not like bagging, packaging, shipping, trips to the post office etc., you will love dealing with digital information. These are good reasons for dealing with digital information products. It is free shipping. Your customer can download your product, you can send it to them by email or other means. They can even look it up in your web site. Another good benefit for dealing with digital information products is that you do not need a space, garage or warehouse because there is nothing to store. You do not have inventory, everything is stored in computers and servers. You do not even need to do anything physical like carrying or lifting. Another good reason is that they are easy to produce if you have a good brain. You do not need expensive equipment, tools or even start up money. All you need is good ideas and the ability to present these ideas in an acceptable and usable form.

If you have the good ideas but you do not have the skills to present them, you can partner with someone who has these skills. If you do not like partnership, you can hire someone who can put your ideas to work. Another good thing about digital information is that your customer doesn't have to wait for the Postman. The customer will get what he wants immediately and that is great because people are inpatient these days. They want everything now. Best of all you can make a sale while you are in bed, the computer does all the work for you. We are living in the age of automation. You can completely automate sales, delivery and even payment 24 hours a day, 7 days a week.

Digital information can be sold in different formats and you can sell them even if you do not have a web site. One way is to make eBooks and sell them on web sites like Amazon.com, clickbank.com and others. I do not advocate selling them on eBay because eBay charge you money to list your items and selling eBooks is not an easy task and in most cases you end up losing money to eBay. I give you an example. If you list say 10 copies of eBook on eBay, you will pay a listing fee on 10 items. This fee is nonrefundable. You pay it whether your item sells or not. Your best chance is that one of these items will sell, the rest will not. That is why when listing any product of digital information, list them in a site that does not charge any listing fee like ioffer.com. You do not need a web site of your own to do that.

Another way to sell digital information is to have a web site that is filled up with useful and usable information that people need real bad, and you charge an annual membership fee just to access your web site and use that information. You can have a web site that has all kinds of legal forms that your customers can print or fill up and submit and you charge money for that. You can make reports that are sold either on your web site or on other web sites like Amazon.com. I will have a separate chapter about how you can sell on Amazon.com. You can have a web site that is offering courses on a specific subject. Restrict yourself to one area of interest, so you can have specific loyal audience. Have like 4 courses, the first course is free, the second is introductory, the third is intermediate and the fourth is advanced. The free course is your best marketing tool, make sure it is excellent and it only covers a very little area of what you are offering. The possibilities are endless. The big question is how to find great ideas that can sell. The first thing to do is to have a little thinking. Ask yourself this question, " Why do people buy? ".

The answer is to satisfy a need or to make their lives easier. Always carry a pen and a piece of paper in your pocket. When you get something in mind, write it down immediately, because good ideas are like alcohol, they evaporate fast. Make a list of the possibilities and always have the competition in your mind. May be you come up with something excellent, but the market is already oversaturated with that thing. Go to eBay and check what people are selling over there and who is buying what. Also, go to a web site called clickbank.com which is specialized in selling digital information products. Look and check what is selling.

If you get an idea and you can not put it in writing, you can find help. Act as soon as you can, before your idea gets out of date or somebody else copies your idea and presents it to the market faster than you do.

One last problem that you have to deal with is the fact that sometimes you need to transfer some big files to your customers. Files that have a lot of graphics and pictures sometimes get too big. Also, audio and video files are very big. Normally, when you send a file through email, you send it as an attachment. There is a limit to how big a file you can send through email as an email attachment. Many corporate email accounts limit attachments to 5MB while free email programs will give you only 5 to maximum of 20 MB. Microsoft and Yahoo's limits are 10 MB. AOL email limit is 16 MB and Google's Gmail is 20 MB. That is enough to send a small group of photos, PDFs or graphic files which leads to frustrated customers due to slow download. So, email is rarely an option when you have a big file to send to your customers because email boxes have attachment size limits. Fortunately, there is a solution. Thanks to the falling prices and costs of bandwidth and the evolution of speedier Internet connections, a host of companies offering file transfer services have emerged. They offer bigger file transfer at lower prices. The services eliminate the need for traditional email attachments. Instead, you upload material to the service which sends a link and not the actual file to the recepients who can then download it for themselves.

One of the best companies that is offering this service for years now is http://www.YouSendIt.Com. This web site is offering a way to get your video clips, music files and huge photos or graphic files to friends and clients without clogging up email boxes. You simply upload the material to the site and it takes care of the rest. The service is free for files up to 100 megabytes or $9.99 a month for files up to 2 gigabytes.

The demand for file transfer services is growing up because file sizes are growing up fast. Digital cameras with big megapixels and high resolution translate into bigger file sizes for photos. Homemade videos are growing up in popularity and people are sending video clips everywhere. Video files are huge.

Other companies are offering the same services. Some of them are:

Http://www.DropSend.Com

Http://www.MediaFire.Com

Http://www.SendSpace.Com

Http://www.TransferBigFiles.Com.

And others. You can do a search and check them out. Go to Google and search for them by writing queries like " big email attachment" , " send big files", or "file transfer service". All of these web sites work almost the same. You need to register for the site first. This is free. Most of these web sites offer a limited free plan and charge for bigger files. See for yourself, if you are sending a file with a size that is within the limit of the free offer, then just use the free service.

Chapter 17

Making Money With eBooks

What is an eBook? An eBook is nothing more than an electronic version of a book, catalog, report or any other publication that is normally published in hard copy. There is no doubt that eBooks are getting more popular day after day. The reason for that is the fact that Internet broadband is almost everywhere now, more popular than ever and does not cost too much as it used to be. Also, what has contributed to the popularity of eBooks is the fact that a lot of handheld mobile devices are already available. These handheld mobile devices have the ability to display eBooks. Also, hardcopy books have problems of their own. They cost more money to produce, they are more expensive to buy, they take a lot of shelf space, they are heavy to carry and they are subject to tear and loss with continual usage. Also do not forget that the World is going green. Cutting on hardcopy books means saving more trees.

A lot of schools are adopting the trend of replacing those heavy textbooks with just a Notebook PC with all the textbooks loaded on the hard drive as eBooks. This trend is spreading fast. Everybody should know that eBooks are more practical and offer a lot of advantages over traditional books. For example, if you are looking for a special topic in a hard cover book, you may have to go through all the pages trying to collect as much information as you can to get a complete answer to your question. Many eBooks contain hyperlinks that make it much easier for you to research the information you are looking for and then return to the place you started to continue reading. Also, a good thing about eBooks is that they can have links to web pages and other interactive features such as audio, video and animation. If you have a Personal Digital Assistant (PDA) or Smart Phone you can have access to all the eBooks that are available. You can also easily transfer the same eBooks to your Notebook or Desktop PC if you would like to.

Text –to-speech technology is available now. Text-to-speech technology enables you to automatically convert any eBook into an audio book that you can listen to from your computer or your PDA. This is a great thing if you are driving and you want to listen to a special eBook. It is also great if you have a problem reading text on a screen. A good thing is that eBooks are available Online immediately and all the time. You do not have to make a trip to the library or to the bookstore. You do not have to wait for the Postal Service to deliver your book.

Before you start dealing with eBooks, you need to have an idea about what they look like first. There are 1000s of eBooks that are available Online for free. The first place to check is the University of Virginia's free eBook Library. Another place is the Microsoft Reader Catalog. A third place is Free-eBooks.net. Once you went to these sites and check out how an eBook looks like, you need something to display them. This is called an eBook reader. There are many eBook readers. The problem with them is that they are not compatible with each other. They use different format that may or may not work for each eBook. If you try to use a different reader for an eBook, it will not display properly. The most important eBook reader is the Microsoft Reader. It is one of many eBooks Readers. Your first step is to download and install Microsoft Reader. It is a piece of software that is free to download. Once you have Microsoft Reader installed on your computer you will be able to read eBooks as soon as you download them. To install it all you need is to go to the Microsoft Reader web site. Once you are on that web site, select "Downloads" then select and click " Reader for Desktop and Laptop PC". To open an eBook, just click its title. The cover page displays briefly and then the first page of the book appears. One of the benefits of an eBook over a traditional hard cover book is the ability to jump logically from one topic or page to the next via hyperlinks. There are lots of functions associated with eBook Reader. For example, if the font size is too small you can change it to a bigger font size so you will be able to read. You can create book marks. You can add margin notes. You can also search for content within an eBook. Practice makes perfect. Before you start making your own eBooks, look at all the details. Look at how other people are creating their own eBooks and always have a pen and a piece of paper. The eBooks that you are going to create need to look professional and have great content. Practice with the Microsoft Reader so you get familiar with it. Try to get some information about other eBook Readers and their formats. Once you know what you getting yourself into, the next step is how to create your own eBooks. You need first to do a market research to know which topics are hot sales and which topics are in high demand. Your eBooks should fill a need, you do not want to waste the time of audience or generate a lot of mistrust. To start creating your own eBooks, you need to install and download another piece of software, an add-on to Microsoft Reader called Read in Microsoft Reader. It is a free program available on the Microsoft eBook Reader web site. Go to the Microsoft eBook Reader home page the click the " For Developer " menu on the left side of the screen, and then select " Read in Microsoft Reader ". Click the " Download Read in Microsoft Reader " link and on the resulting web page click the " WordRHE.exe " link then follow the instructions. Once you have that piece of software installed on your computer, you can create and publish you're your own eBook. You also need Microsoft word. You have to create your eBook in Microsoft Word first. After you finished creating your eBook in Microsoft Word, all you have to do is to click the " Read in Microsoft Reader " icon, then your eBook is now published.

Once you have your eBook created, it is time to make it available to your customers and to figure out how to make money with it. You have two choices. The first and most important choice is to make it available for download. The easiest way to make your eBook available for download is to submit it to an electronic bookstore. Make a search on the web and get results. Each site has its own rules for submitting content so be sure to research several sites before deciding where to offer your eBook to your customers. You will want to find the ones that best serve your target readers. The second choice is that if you have a web site you can make eBook available on your web site and if you are selling it on eBay, provide a link to your web site so your customers can go and download it. To make your eBook available on your web site, you need first to upload the eBook files to your web server, then set the permission on the files to 755 or 644, depending on your server settings then create a hyperlink to the file at the appropriate place on your web site.

There is no doubt that eBooks can be money makers if you know how to do it right. You need to choose the right topic, be professional and adopt a good marketing plan.

If you have a hard time selling your eBook, do as what some other web sites are doing; offer it for free to those who visit your web site and do something like register, sign up or buy anything. Usually people come to your web site if you are offering something of value for free. A good thing to offer for free is your eBook. It does not cost you too much and at the same time it can help you build a good customer base and even an email list. The content of your eBook should have something to do with your main web site activity. For example, if you are selling memberships for customers to lose weight, your eBook can be about healthy foods, healthy diets and so on.

Chapter 18

Making Money with Online Self Publishing

Writing a book is much easier than you think. A lot of people do not believe the fact that the information industry amounts now to more than half of the U.S. Gross National Income. There is no doubt that when it comes to information, there is lots of money to be made. Publishing a book is part of that spectrum. A book can bring you not only fame but also wealth. You can all of a sudden become a celebrity author for one reason or another. Writing a book can help you establish yourself as a master in your field. People have that false idea that they need to have a doctoral degree to be able to write a book. Becoming an expert in your field does not require a great education or even a college degree. You can become an expert in a very small area if you are willing to go deep into that area. All it takes is hard work, research the Internet which is considered the largest library in the world and read about your subject as much as you can. Do not forget to write down the important information you collect about your subject.

In the Internet age, anyone can be an author. Best of all, you can cut the middleman and pocket most of the profit. Large publishers are not interested whether your book is a good book. All they want to know is whether it will sell. Therefore, they concentrate their efforts on well known authors with good track records. If you are just a new author you could not approach large publishers but this now has changed thanks to the Internet which introduced what is called on demand publishing. On demand publishing means that your book is only produced when it is ordered. Also, the author royalty now is much more than it used to be. The author used to get a royalty from the large publishers of 6 to 10% of the net receipts. Now, it is about 40% or more thanks to the Internet Publishing Companies which I will tell you about later in this chapter.

With self publishing you can make more money, you can publish your book faster and you can have more control on your book. Computerized equipment allows people to rapidly write, edit, layout, print and deliver books.

If you decide to write a book, you should write on a subject you like. You should write on a subject you are good at. You should write on a subject that can sell. Most often the subject of the book, not the name of the author or publisher, is what makes the book sell. How to subjects in general, have the best sales potential, followed by self improvement subjects, hobbies, health and sex, money and business and psychological well being. The best thing is to find a need and try to fill it. Try to remember that most people buy nonfiction books hoping to learn something or solve a problem. You are writing your book to help them.

Although writing a book is not difficult, it is not for the lazy. Once you select a topic, try to set up a writing area in a spare room or even a corner in the living or dining room. Stay away from the bedroom. A good title is a must. It is the best sale pitch. More than half of your sales will be based upon your title. If you have a poor title your book will be passed unnoticed. If you have a poor title, customers will never think of your book as valuable. It is hard to sell a book with poor title. Make a list of the best possible titles for your book and consult with relatives and friends then choose the best of the best. Your title should be short, catchy and descriptive. You can add a subtitle to it. The subtitle should give the potential reader more details about the contents of your book in an attractive way. The title should have big letters, the subtitle is done with smaller letters. I usually choose my books depending on how attractive the title is. Books with poor titles, I always ignore them.

The book's cove includes the front cover, the back cover and the spine. You front cover should feature the title and the subtitle. The back cover should contain a summary of the benefits of reading this book or some testimonials. It has to speak to the potential buyer. The spine should have the title on it written clearly so it will read easily on the shelf. Since most of the books are ordered now online, that spine thing is not so essential.

Finding material for your book is not that hard. All your research efforts should begin with the Internet because there is already huge amount of information and the good thing is that the information is continuously updated. Try to gather everything that is written on your subject. The golden rule is: Copying ideas is research, copying words is plagiarism. So copy ideas, copy facts but do not copy words. Organize your materials into notes then make a chapter of your notes and so on.

Most Internet Publishing sites require that you upload your files in PDFs. This is done using software called Adobe Acrobat. If you do not have Adobe Acrobat you need to buy one. Few of these companies accept Microsoft files. The best way to write your book is to use Microsoft Word which has a lot of great features and very easy to use. When you finish, you can transfer your files very easily into PDFs either using the Adobe Acrobat or an add-on software available for free download from Microsoft. When it comes to designing your book, the standard trim size could be 5.5 inches by 8.5 inches or 8.5 inches by 11 inches. As for the number of pages your aim should be between 144 and 288 total interior pages to be in the best economical point of view. If your book has just 90 pages (2x45) you can not get the price you want out of it. A book of more than 800 pages will cost more money to produce because of the price of papers.

A good book cover protects the contents of the book and can help you sell the book. The front cover should include the title and subtitle, name of the author and a related photograph or drawing that has impact and can attract book readers to have a look at your book. The front cover can be a very big sales tool for your book. The spine of the book usually has the title of the book, the name of the author and an eye catching symbol or icon that used to attract buyers in the old good days. The back cover may have something about the author e.g. his background if he is famous or his photo if he is a good looking. If you do not have either, you can just put something to promote the book like a summary of the best points in the book or some good testimonials. Also in the back cover is the ISBN of the book, you can not sell the book without having an ISBN number. Also, the back cover has the price of the book.

The wave of the future is pint on demand. That means every book that is printed is already sold. In the old good days, you used to print a couple thousand copies at once. There is no guarantee that you will be able to sell them all. So, you end up with a lot of unsold copies. This will eat up a big part of your profits. With that new print on demand trend, all your copies are guaranteed to sell. This will translate into higher profits. A good thing in your side these days is the fact that there is now a growing number of Internet based publishing companies that are practically do most of the work for you. They publish your book, market your book and sell it, even they collect the money for you. Your start up money is almost nothing. All you need to do is to sit down and write your book. In the past, it used to cost you a lot of money upfront to get your book published because you have to pay for a certain amount of copies. Things have changed now. You do not have to buy or pay anything. I made my own research on the Internet to find the good available companies which do on demand publishing for two reasons. The first reason is to finish up this chapter and the second reason is to find a good company to publish this book. I found a lot of good companies on the Internet. The best two, in my opinion, are:

Http://www.CreateSpace.Com

Http://www.Lulu.Com

I will give details for the purpose of this book about the first one. It is up to you to check the others and choose what you think is the best for you. A piece of advice, whatever company you choose, marketing your book is your responsibility. So, you need to choose a company that gives you more control over your book in a way that it allows you to have more avenues to sell your book.

If you are serious this opportunity can be a good money maker. You do not need to have your own web site to sell your book. You can make money with your book without having a web site, so this opportunity is for everyone. All you need to have is a computer, a good idea and a no lazy attitude.

Http://www.CreateSpace.com

This web site offers you free Online Publishing tools and community that can help you complete and sell your work. You can distribute your book on Amazon.com, your own web site and other retailer channels without set up fee or inventory. You can make your titles available to millions of customers on Amazon.Com and other channels. Set up is free with createspace.com free tools, and you will never have to worry about inventory or minimum orders.

There is no set up fees for your book before making it available for sale. The only requirement for you is to purchase and approve a proof copy of your book. The web site will also provide you with a free createSpace ISBN if you do not already have one. If you do not already own an ISBN the site will automatically assign one to your book. The ISBN assigned to your book by createSpace.com is a valid ISBN purchased from the U.S. ISBN agency, R.R. BowKer. This ISBN belongs to createSpce.com and can not be used to publish the book with another publisher. There is no additional charge for the assignment of an ISBN to your book.

All books must be a minimum of 24 pages. The maximum number of pages you can have vary by trim size and printing options. To sell your title on a createSpace public E-store and/or the Amazon Retail program you must specify the retail price during the title set up. List price is your suggested retail price or MSRP. Your book will be printed on demand, after a customer orders, using the latest digital printing available. Your book's interior will be produced in full color or black and white, depending upon the option you have selected. All book covers are printed in full color on cover stock and finished with a protective laminated coating. The web site member agreement requires that you own or have obtained all rights to any content you deliver to CreatSpace.Com (no one will violates your intellectual property rights.). All files must be submitted as PDFs through the CreateSpace.Com web site. The cover file for your book should not exceed 40 MB, the interior file for your book should not exceed 100 MB. When your book files meet all requirements, you will need to order a proof copy which CreateSpace.Com will then print and ship to you.

A CreateSpace E-store is a customizable sales page that allows you to sell directly to customers. There is no charge to set up an E-store for your title. E-store includes a customizable banner and description, promotional clip hosting as well as background and text colors of your choice. Each title you publish through CreateSpace.Com can have its own unique E-store. Just link to the E-store's URL from your site and include the URL in emails to prospective customers.

Chapter 19

Your Own Blog

A weblog or blog is a web site that is designed to enable you to write entries for others to view. Most of the blogs have the tools to let the viewers leave their comments on these entries. While entries are displayed in chronological order, comments are shown in reverse chronological order. Visitors to your blog view your entry and the most recent comment at the top of the page. If they want, they can scroll down to read the entire thread of comments.

Blogs have become very popular, so popular that almost every Internet user not only has heard of them but probably has actually visited some of them. Blogs are extending to almost every area of our lives such as news, food, sports, health, arts etc. The number of active blogger is exploding to more than 35 millions in the U.S. alone. Different search engines pay a lot of attention to blogs because their contents are always updated. When blogs started few years ago, they were intended to like personal web sites. But very soon, different companies and organizations have realized the full potential of blogging, so most companies, organizations and even the governments have their own blogs now. The goal is clear; to share information, to reach more audience and to use them as a marketing tool.

Most of the blogs are made up of text, but advances in technology have led to the creation of what is called Rich Media Blogs. Rich Media Blogs are just regular blogs that have audio and video content in addition to the regular text. You do not need to have a web site to create your own blog. There are lots of web sites that offer their audience a free blog. That is the easiest way to get into the world of blogging and start practicing. It does not cost you anything. It is free and you do not have to be a blog expert to create it. They made it very simple for you, even a child can do it on his own.

One of the most popular sites that is offering free blogs is http://www.blogger.com. The first thing you need to do is to sign up for a free account, then you can create your own weblog in very few easy steps. Once you publish your own blog, readers can comment on what you have posted. This is called feedback. You have the choice to accept or reject that feedback. You can reject it if you think it is a negative comment and will not support your goal. You can even delete any comments you do not like and that is a good thing. The bad thing about free blogs is that you can hardly make money of them. You do not have a lot of control on your blog. Some hosts will put ads in your site and there are limitations when it comes to disk space and band usage. The worst thing is that you can not have your own domain. With all these limitations, you can still make some money and it can be a good learning experience for you to have your own standalone blog.

If you are serious about making money with a blog, get your own domain and create your own blog. There are lots of web hosting companies that offer a platform that lets you create and manage your own blog. They have the software to let you do that. This is the best approach. It is very cost effective. If you want to host your blog on your own server, you need special software to do that and you need to have the required skills to set up and run a server. The most popular blogging software is Wordpress.

For your weblog to take off and successful, you need to select your topic carefully. There are lots of topics that are hot among people like photography, video, health issues etc. After you choose your topic, try to narrow it. For example, if your topic is photography, to narrow it, try to discuss only digital cameras and so on. The more specific you are, the more loyal audience you will get. At the time the search engines will consider your blog seriously and you will get a high ranking among search engines. There are other things that your weblog must have to grow successful. The first thing you must have is high quality content. Make sure that the contents of your blog are of top quality, are useful and have something that people would love to know about. For example, if your blog is about a product, include useful tips about how to use this product, safety tips, information that can help your customers better understand your product and so on. Try to include all this information in a very funny and entertaining way so your customers do not get bored. You can post and ask challenge questions to get your customers' attention and participation. The second thing that your weblog must have is a new content. You should post new entries on a regular basis. It is best to do it weekly.

You should know that visiting a blog with old entries is exactly like reading an old newspaper. Your visitors will stop coming back if there is nothing new. The third thing that your blog must have is to let your readers leave their comments. That is very important if you want to keep loyal audience. A one-side communication is not interesting at all. It is generally unacceptable in the world of blogging. Establishing a two way communication will not only give your blog a new life but also help you get valuable information from the comments of your audience. Readers' feedback is very important. You can even go further concerning that subject. Some readers may want to contact you directly instead of leaving a comment on your blog. Give them the opportunity to do this by including your email address. You can also add a contact page. You can build a community by including links to other blogs discussing the same topic. This will enrich your weblog and establish you as an expert on the subject. If you are writing about a variety of topics you can include tags on the side that people can click to go to what they want on your weblog. Also offer an RSS feed subscription which allows users to subscribe. This ensures that the blog readers get the latest updates in the most convenient way. Letting your readers here from you often and encouraging your audience to subscribe via RSS are key ingredients in gathering interest that keeps readers come back for more. Most weblog sites now offer you the option of including an RSS feed. Blogger.com gives you that choice. They even go further. They make you decide how much of your content you want to syndicate. They offer you three choices. The first one is full which means you choose to syndicate the whole post. The second choice is short which means you choose to syndicate part, usually the beginning of the post. The third choice is non which means you choose to turn off the site feed completely.

Now the most important question of the chapter is: How can you make money with a blog?

The first thing you can do to make money with your blog is to try to sell your expertise. Having a popular weblog means you have two skills: You are an expert blogger and you are an expert in the topic of your blog. You can capitalize on this. This option is available to every blogger even if you only have a free blog. You have a chance to be a celebrity in your field. You can market these two skills and your new status any way you like. There are unlimited opportunities e.g. consultant, writer to other blogs, giving speeches and seminars etc. You need to realize the full potential of the blogs; they are the wave of the future.

A second way to make money with your blog is to sell a product or service. That product or service should be related to your topic. This option is available only to those who host their own blog. If you have a free weblog, you can not do this. Since you are selling only one product or a very limited number of products, you only need to have the PayPal Payment System which is totally free. It is a great way of making money. Think of anything you can sell that is related to your topic.

Another way to make money with a blog is through accepting advertising in your blog. A very common way to make money advertising is to sign up for Google Adsense. It is a very successful program and very easy to set up and implement. This option is available even to those with free blogs.

Another good way to make money with your blog is to join affiliate programs. This option is also available to those with free blogs. Affiliation programs are so important that I will discuss them in a separate chapter.

The last way to make money with your blog is to sell it to someone or some company who is interested in it, then you start all over again.

Chapter 20

Podcasting For Cash

In this chapter I will discuss what podcasting is, how it is done and how you can make money with it. A lot of people think that podcasting is nothing more than just a downloadable audio or video file that is Online. Podcasting is much more than this. With the addition of another component called RSS (Really Simple Syndication), a revolution has happened to podcasting. RSS not only notifies subscribers of new information but also actually delivers it to them ant time they want. RSS is so important that I will discuss it in a separate chapter.

Podcasting is considered a natural extension of blogging. It goes far beyond text and written word. It is the art of making syndicated audio and video available for you to communicate with your audience. There are lots of areas that podcasting can be used for like advertising, education, news, media and public relations and internal communications. Best of all, podcasting is not just for big companies anymore. To have an idea about podcasting, visit the best podcasting web site at http://www.itconversations.com. You will find more than two thousands different podcasts. Audio and video have become a more popular means of sharing information on the Internet, thanks to podcasting and RSS feed. Instead of reading information, you can relax and listen to a podcast even when you are driving. Podcasts are easy to produce. Anyone can create and syndicate a podcast as long as he has some basic equipment and a basic knowledge of RSS. The best thing about podcasting is that it is still so young as an industry so if you jump to it you could be a pioneer. Very soon podcasting will become the new means of sharing information over the web. This means it will open new opportunities for those who are willing to learn.

To produce a podcast, the first step is to select the topic and write the content. The second step is to select your team, those who will help you in the production process. That team can include a lot of people or just you. You need to make sure the host of your podcast has an easy to listen to, professionally sounding voice. If you are producing video podcasts, you should have someone who presents well in front of the camera. The voice should simply easy to listen to, the content has to be good and should be targeting your audience. You should be familiar with the audio and video equipment and how to use them. You need to know how to handle the web publishing and RSS feed component. You can learn how to produce an entire podcast and publish it to the web on your own. All these skills can be acquired by practice. You must know your target audience so you can send them the right message. You need to have a high quality content and to be specific. The most popular format of podcasting is the single host talk. It is less expensive to produce. There are other formats, beyond the scope of this book. The minimum you need to produce your podcast is a microphone and an editing workstation that includes a powerful computer, proper editing software, headphones, speakers and Internet access. Using headphones and speakers allow you to listen to the podcast the ways your listeners would. If you have a quality microphone, it will give a better audio quality. There are plenty of options when it comes to choosing an audio recording software for your podcasting. Prices can range free up to 1000s of dollars. Audacity is a free, open source audio recording and editing software. It is great for beginners. It is available for Windows, Mac and Linux. After you finish recording your podcast, it is time for editing. Editing is important because it will give you a much cleaner podcast. After you complete your editing, you need to format your final audio file. The most popular way to format an audio file is an MP3. Then the last step is to add what is called a metadata. Metadata is the information stored inside the MP3 file about the podcast title, author etc. This will help listeners identify the podcast. Now it is time to publish your podcast. The most popular way is to use a blog. You can also publish your podcast to your web site. It is getting more popular now to have your web site that has a blog and you publish your podcast in that blog.

Now you have your podcast with great content, well produced and ready, it is time to make your customers know about it. That is marketing your podcast. There are lots of things you can do to make people aware of your podcast. Podcasts are usually made in episodes. You do not just produce one and that set. You need to produce them on a regular basis. This can be weekly, biweekly or on a monthly basis. This is the way to do it to be successful. You need to publish them in a prominent place in your web site or blog. Offer your customer more than one option to review your podcast. They can download your podcast or they can listen to your podcast while on your web site or blog. Offer them a way to subscribe to your RSS feed. Submit your podcast to Online Podcast Directories. There are lots of Online Podcast Directories, the most famous of them are Apple itunes and Yahoo. You can also use social network media like facebook.com and myspace.com to publicize your podcast. These sites are used even by the government and they are so popular. There are many other techniques and strategies to market your podcast. It is beyond the scope of this book.

The question now is: How can you make money with your podcast?

If you like this field, you can establish yourself as an expert in the field. There is a lot of money to be made. To establish yourself as an expert is not an easy task. It will take a lot of hard work and practice. Fortunately, we are in the age of the Internet. Information is everywhere and most of that information is free. Collect as much information as you can on the subject. Once you know what you are doing, you can start marketing yourself. The best places to go is to register with http://www.rentAcoder.com and http://www.elance.com. You can advertise yourself in Craig's list. There are lots of companies and organizations that need help to produce their own podcasts for marketing, advertising and communications. You can take full advantage of this. Once you have a good track record, you will have more work than you can handle. You do not need to have a web site to make money with podcasting. But if you are willing to have your own web site, you can make it about the topic of podcasting to provide people with information about podcasting. People who are interested in podcasting will come to your web site and you will have a lot of traffic. This way you can put ads in your web site and also you can get customers at the same time. Adding a podcast to your web site will help you attract more audience to the content of your web site. A good podcast and high quality content can work together to generate income for you.

If you are selling a product on your web site, you still can sell that product with the help of your podcast. You can place commercials and advertisements in your podcast but you have to be careful not to offend your audience.

You can make money with your podcast through the affiliate programs. Affiliate programs now exist for almost every product sold. It is very easy to find products that are a good fit for your audience. Affiliate programs are a good way to make money that I will discuss them in a separate chapter.

Once you establish yourself and build an audience to your episodes of podcasting, you can start charging a modest subscription fee. But you have to make sure that your content is too good and you will not lose your customers by doing something like this.

Another way of making money with podcasts is, of course, to make them and offer them for sale.

Chapter 21

RSS Feed

RSS stands for Really Simple Syndication. This is the technology that has helped all major media outlets take off. RSS has changed the way we deliver content Online especially for audio and video. Thanks to RSS now, all types of content; text, audio, video etc. can be delivered to you. You do not have to listen or watch them immediately. To explain more, it is like a Digital Video Recorder or DVR. When you are at work or busy doing something and there is a show you do not want to miss, you can set up or program your DVR to record the show then you can watch it any time you like. RSS enables you to subscribe to and then automatically download new content every time it is published. You can look at them any time you want.

Thanks to the RSS, blogs are now more popular than ever. There are an estimated more than 80 million blogs worldwide and more are coming every day. Podcasts also are gaining a lot of popularity thanks to the RSS technology. RSS is not just for blogs and podcasts. The technology has been used now by major media outlets, government agencies and corporations to disseminate information. Companies are using the RSS as a way to share company news, product announcements and the other public relations efforts.

The last version of RSS (RSS 2.0) is supported by both Microsoft Windows Vista and all of the major browsers. This means you can very easily subscribe to and view RSS feeds right in your browser. The RSS community has adopted a universal feed icon. When you see this icon in a web site, it tells you that this web site contains RSS feed channels that you can subscribe to.

There are four steps to the RSS syndication. The first step is create the content e.g. a podcast and uploads it as an XML file to the web server. Contained in this file is data about the RSS feed. This is generally includes title, description, author and podcast URL. The second step happens when someone tries to subscribe to your RSS feed by adding the RSS feed URL to the feedreader. A feedreader is a piece of software that allows the end user to subscribe to the RSS feed and check for any updated feed. The most popular feedreader is Google reader. You can get it at http://www.Google.com/reader. **Once a person has subscribed, his feedreader will check the RSS feed at regular intervals for any new content that has been added. The third step happens when the web site author adds new content to the RSS feed file. The fourth step happens when the customer's feedreader software discovers the new content and downloads the updates and marks it as new.**

RSS can be a great marketing tool. It can help you build your audience and help you build a serious email list. The content of your RSS feed should be of high quality and directed to the right audience. Ads should be at minimum so you do not offend your customers.

Chapter 22

Starting a Wiki

A wiki is not as popular as a blog but it is on the way to be popular especially if it is used in a popular way. It is another aspect of what is called Web 2.0. A wiki is a web site you create that enables others to easily read and add information to your web pages. It is a great way to build specific communities. Wikis are becoming increasingly popular to meet education and government goals such as critical thinking, research and collaboration. The popularity of wikis has a lot to do with the Wikipedia web site which everybody is almost familiar with. Wikipedia is an Online encyclopedia that uses the wiki format. You need to go and visit the Wikipedia site to get familiar with it. Although most of the wikis are made by government and educational institutions, you still can have your personal wiki and make money out of it too.

Once you create a wiki, other users can easily make edits to the pages. The edits appear in real time which means they appear instantly. Every edit is stored for the life of the wiki which makes it easy to check to see when a change was made and who made it. You can also remove edits that are incorrect or inappropriate. You can apply passwords to a wiki to restrict edits to certain group of users. You can also block users by IP (Internet Protocol) address and/or username if necessary. Most wikis are based on web servers called wiki engines. There are variety if wiki engines available and most of them provide strong content controls that help you monitor every page in a wiki to ensure quality control. Although a wiki is technically a web site, you do not need any knowledge of HTML (Hypertext Markup Language) programming. HTML is the language that is often used to create web sites. There are some minor text formatting instructions that you need to know but these are quick and easy to learn. You can include many types of elements in most wikis including text, graphics, hyperlinks and other items. You can also apply many levels of security depending on the nature and use of your wiki.

For your wiki to be successful, it needs to have a focus and targeted goal in order for people find what they want and to be always engaged. If the wiki is left open ended people may comment, but some of these contributions probably will not be very pertinent to the topic. Few people want to read a wiki that is just a mix of unrelated topics. Thus your goal is to create a wiki that has a specific topic and a specific content. This will be your big step to create a common link to a successful community building. When starting your wiki you need to consider what your main purpose will be. You need to consider if your wiki will be for documentation, event planning, information building etc. The possibilities are almost endless and your ultimate goal is to build a community around your wiki.

Before launching your own wiki, check out several different examples of them in addition to the Wikipedia. Look for examples of different formats, methods and means. Seeing them used in different ways will help you decide how you want to shape your wiki. Check out http://www.wikia.com for a directory of wikis on a variety of subjects.

Your wiki can be either open for anyone to edit or secure and limited to contributions by registered users. Limiting access to your wiki can sometimes generate better content, and encourage other visitors to check out your wiki but open access allows others to engage in your community and possibly be converted to a subscriber. You need to choose what best works for you and your audience and determine the level of participation that is available based on that decision. If you choose to limit wiki participation to subscribers only, it may be a good idea to require that a contributor's name to be attached to a port, article or revision. This will clearly identify the contributors and force them to consider their words just as much as if they were speaking with colleagues. The first step in getting people engaged in your wiki after you launch it is to let your audience familiarize themselves with the space and to register in the wiki if they are going to participate. You want to give your participants a sense of ownership so as to foster greater loyalty. If your participants feel that they have a stake in the wiki, they will take pains to ensure the accuracy of the information that is shared and the maintenance and provision of information. After you start promoting the fact that you have launched a wiki, it becomes time to start building the content that will foster participation and help your community grow. At first your wiki will be clean with no content. It will most likely fall on you to take the initial steps and post the initial content. Fortunately for you, deciding on your content should not be too challenging, since it should be relevant to the content you have in mind at the beginning of the planning period. For instance, if your original plan is about marketing strategies for antique dealers, you can start developing content on how to start generating new inventory or even posting the tips you describe as text. Once the initial content is posted, you can start building momentum and participation by hosting collaborative events. These " born – raising " events are a great way to familiarize your audience with your wiki and create the mass content that appeal to future community members. An additional benefit to organizing a collaborative event for your wiki is that it gets the community off and running as individuals to work to support and assist one another in the creation of content. Bear in mind that although most people today are familiar with what a wiki is, many are not familiar with how to edit and participate with them. You need at the beginning to help your community learn and grow their confidence. Not everyone will amount to or be able to participate in a collaborative session for your wiki. Still inviting your audience to explore and contribute is a fantastic way to begin audience engagement.

Wikis are a great way to help others have their own wikis. Another approach for making money with a wiki is to have a wiki that is part of your nonprofit organization. You can have a wiki that, for example, teaches poor people new skills as part of your nonprofit organization and you can invite everyone who has a skill to participate. You can have a wiki that is specialized in collecting data or making surveys.

You can also make money with your wiki by accepting advertising.

Finally, you need to do more research if you are interested in wikis. The more research you do, the more ideas you will be getting.

Chapter 23

Selling Domains

Do you know that there are thousands of people in this country who are making a living buying and selling domains, most of them are doing it on a part time basis. You can be one of these people, there is nothing wrong with this. You do not need to have your own web site to sell domains. All you need to have is a computer with Internet connection. You can even use the computer in your public library. You can register a domain for years without having a web site for it. This is called domain parking. During that period of time you can turn around and sell your domain to someone who is interested in it. The domain business used to be very hot but it has settled down. It will take you more time to sell a domain with the price you want. Still there is a lot of money to be made and the return on your investment is huge. For example, if you registered a domain for $10.00 a year and you sold it for $100.00, you made 10 times worth your initial investment. Sometimes you get very lucky when someone happens to be crazy about your domain and offers you thousands of dollars for it. It looks like hitting the lottery. Some domains e.g. sex.com, blue.com etc. were sold for millions of dollars. The bad thing about this kind of business is that most of the good domains are gone. I mean they are already registered to somebody else. The best you can do is to start buying them for cheap and sell them high. If you have some marketing skills you can do very well in this field. To succeed in this business, you need to register as many good domains as you can. For example, if you register 10 domains your chance of selling one of them at a reasonable price is better than if you register only one. Domain registration is a very easy and straightforward process. To do it right, you need to make a long list of possible good names. The next step is to go to a web site like Yahoo.com and check if any of these domains is available. If you find one or few of them are available, do not wait, just register them immediately. Waiting even few minutes can cost you the loss of the domains. You will find these domains are already gone. It will take a lot of hours, may be days or weeks to register something decent, so you need to be patient. Another good source to buy and register domains is what is called after market domains. These are good domains that people registered and forgot about them, so they go for auctions in places like Godaddy.com. You can go after them because some of them are actually good domains and have a lot of potential. Another source of good domains is eBay auctions. I found a lot of good domains listed on eBay for a very decent starting price. By any means, if you are serious you need to start having your own collection of domains. It is not expensive to register a domain for a whole full year. I own a lot of domains and I am not worried about selling them because I know that year after year they go up in value. It is like real estate market, location, location, location. Something like this applies to domains. Every property is unique and has its own value, so is every domain. There are good domains and bad ones and no two domains are alike. As I said the best thing about the domain business is that you do not need too much capital to get started and also you do not need your own web site. You can start small by registering few domains and once you sell some of them you can buy or register some more and so on.

I talked before in this book about what makes a good domain. You can go back and read that chapter. I do not want to repeat. Now, we come to the important part which is how you can sell your domain. The first thing I want to warn you of is the fact that as soon as the domain business starts to take off, there are other businesses that came to life to suck you in and make you spend more money. I will give you a lot of examples just to make you more cautious. There are some companies that are offering what is called domain appraisal. They charge you a lot of money just to tell you what your domain is worth. This is one example of unnecessary expenses and you do not need to pay for this. You already have an idea in your mind about the value of your domain. If you do not know, just go to any web site that is listing domains for sale and an idea about what your domain could be worth. Other web sites that are specialized in listing domains for sale are offering free listing and what they call featured listing. They claim that featured listing will enhance your chance of selling your domain. Featured listing costs a lot of money and there is no guarantee that your domain will sell. In most cases you end up losing more money. What I do I list my domains in the free category. If they sell, that is fine. If they do not sell, I am not losing anything. The idea is not to pay a dime over that $10.00 you spend to register your domain. You have to put in your mind that it can take you years to sell a domain. You have to understand how domains are sold. Those companies who list domains for sale do not have good track records of how many domains they actually sold out of the hundreds of thousands of domains that are currently on their lists. I think it much less than one percent. What they do is just list those domains without doing any effort to market them. If a domain is sold by chance, they not only get credit for it but they also get at least a 20% of the sale price for practically doing nothing. So, you are better off selling your domain on your own. If you list your domains with them make sure of two things. The first thing is the price of your domain. Make sure your price is made up of your asking price plus their commission. The second thing is to make sure that you have the right to sell your domain somewhere else anytime and you pay them nothing. Most of the domains are sold this way:

Suppose you are starting a company and you are trying to register a domain that you think it is a good fit for your business. You find out that this domain is unavailable. Since you fall in love with this domain, you go to Whois.com web site to check about the owner. You negotiate with the owner for a price to the domain. All of a sudden you get an email from someone who is interested in offering you some money for your domain. Another active way to sell your domain is to make a list of companies that you think they will benefit from buying your domain. Most of these companies have web sites with bad domains. You contact them and tell them that you have a great domain that is much better than the one they have and you are ready to sell it to them for a reasonable price. You mention to them the benefits that they will get by acquiring this domain. If you are willing to accept a lower price for your domain or you are in a hurry to sell, you can list your domain on eBay. I list my domains on eBay the smart way. Many times, usually once a month or every other month, eBay send an email for its members offering them free listing on a certain day. I usually take advantage of this opportunity and list all my domains with the best asking price that I am looking for. It is a free listing. If your item sells, it is great and you pay eBay their standard fees. If your item doesn't sell, you do not lose any money. That is the way I do it because there is no guarantee that your item will sell even in auctions. The people who are serious about that business usually register more than one thousand domains. If you manage to sell even one percent of them, you still can make money and profit. Some people even go all the way by setting up a web site that specializes in selling domains and list his domains in addition to other people's domains. I will have a separate chapter about how you can set up a web site that deals with domains. One more tip I want to mention is that when you register a domain you have the chance to keep your information private or public. If you choose to keep your information private, your chance of selling your domain will be decreased. There will be no way for potential buyers to know who owns that domain. When People usually go to Whois.com to check on the domain owner, they get no contact information. So, when you register a domain, make sure that your information is public. This way a prospective buyer can contact you. If you do not want to disclose your private email, have a Yahoo email and check your email on a regular basis.

Another tip I want to tell you about is that if it happen that you sold a domain for a lot of money e.g. thousands of dollars, you need to finalize your deal with what is called an escrow account. An escrow account is a great thing for both the buyer and you too. You only get your money after safely transfer the domain to the buyer. At the same time the buyer can not touch that money or get it back if he already received the domain. It can protect both of you against fraud. However, there is no need for this service if you are selling a domain for a small amount of money e.g. a hundred dollars.

If you receive an offer that is far below the asking price, do not give up. Make a counter offer, and remind the potential buyer of how valuable your domain will be for him or her. You need to know that in most cases you will never get what you are asking for when it comes to domain selling, unless your domain is so unique and the buyer wants it real bad or there is a lot of competition for acquiring your domain. How much you can give up, depends on you and your domain.

A final thought is that there are lots of web sites that are dealing with domains, try to pay them a visit on a regular basis. The more you go over there, the more you learn.

Chapter 24

Selling Web Sites

Have you ever thought about selling a whole web site?! This can be a very lucrative business. It has been done every day. Just go to eBay and have a look. You will see hundreds of web sites listed for sale in auctions. Probably the first thing that will come to your mind is to reject the idea simply because you do not know how to build them and you are not that kind of a tech guy. You do not have to be a web designer or a web developer to tap into that field. All you have to do is to try to partner with somebody who knows how to build web sites. You can even partner with a young high School kid who is interested in this kind of stuff and you are in business. You will be amazed of how much these young kids can do. You give him the idea of your web site or your project. You can pay him by the project or you give him part of the proceeds of the sale. The good thing about the young high school kid is that he will not ask for too much. He will be happy with what he gets. He knows how to build web sites for the fun of it or to prove himself, but he doesn't know how to market them. There are unlimited ideas for a web site. You do not want to build a primitive web site and try to offer it for sale. It will not sell. You need to be highly professional. It will be a good idea to offer a detailed guide with every web site you are offering for sale. This guide will be generic and designed to educate your customer on topics like how to maintain a web site, search engine optimization, how to market your web site and other topics that will help your customer get a return on his investment. Offer your customer unlimited consultation for at least three months. You do not want your customer to fail. Do whatever you can to make him feel that he made a good investment.

If it happens that you are a web developer or working in the field of building web sites, it could be even better for you. At least, you can keep all the profit for yourself. You can even take your business a step further. Build your own web server and host all the web sites you build and offer for sale. After selling a web site you give the buyer the option to keep you as a hosting company for a reasonable monthly fee. To sweeten the deal, you can offer one year free hosting. So you can make money from selling web sites and hosting at the same time. You will have a monthly income for the life of the web site you sold especially if you are offering good customer service and reasonable prices. A good customer service is the rule because the competition is very tough among hosting companies. There are lots of technical figures who are doing this and they are making lots of money. If you are a regular guy with no money or technical skills, you can still be able to do it. Just do not forget the young high school kid that you are going to partner with.

Chapter 25

PayPal

PayPal is considered one of the best acquisition that has been made by eBay. PayPal which is considered a key growth factor for eBay, is quickly establishing itself as a global payment processor and as the largest player focused solely on online payment. The PayPal brand now stands side to side with dominant payment brands like Visa, Master Card, American Express and Discover. Millions of users are now using PayPal as a trusted brand for facilitating online payments. The unprecedented success of PayPal is due to the fact that its platform was built with E-Commerce in mind. It has developed the tools to facilitate and simplify the unique complexities of handling card payment over the web which is considered one of the fastest growth categories in payment. The online businesses and sellers benefit from this simplification in several ways:

1. Ease of use:
   PayPal gives virtually anyone the capacity to accept payments. There are no minimum requirements for payment volume to use PayPal.

2. High level of trust:
   PayPal has encouraged the use of online payment by lowering users' safety concerns and raising their willingness to send money online.

What is so great about PayPal is the fact that it is different from other payment brands e.g. Master Card & Visa in that it is considered a single source provider of payment services. Small merchants can sign up for PayPal Merchant Services and get all of their payment needs. They do not practically need to have a separate merchant bank account or a payment gateway services provider.

PayPal is gradually expanding its presence beyond eBay. Basically, it is now offering several different ways for payment acceptance based on the size and needs of the merchant.

1. Email Payments:

This is the offering used largely by smaller eBay and non eBay merchants who receive payments entirely via email. These usually do not have web sites to integrate with PayPal.

2. Web Site Payment Standard:

   This service allows merchants to place a PayPal button on their site and when a user is ready to check out, the user hits the button and is taken to the PayPal site where the actual check out takes place.

3. Web Site Payment Pro:

   This service is intended for small to medium size sellers. The site should have a shopping cart that is compatible with PayPal. Actually, most of the shopping carts are compatible but it doesn't hurt to ask to make sure that your shopping cart is compatible. This service provides better integration but there is a monthly fee of $30.00.

4. Express Checkout:

   This service is intended for larger merchants e.g. Dell. When a shopper uses Express Checkout, he logs into PayPal and PayPal then forwards address and other information to the merchant. The good thing about this whole process is the fact that it allows an existing PayPal user to bypass entering personal and shipping information again, even if it is the user's first time using that specific merchant. It is considered another payment acceptance service used by the vendor and it gives the user an additional checkout option.

PayPal is also offering other services that are helping both sellers and buyers and it is regularly adding more services.

If you have not yet been a member of PayPal, please, do register as soon as you can. You do not need to have a web site to be a member. All you need to have is a valid address, a valid email and a checking account. This is your first step to the world of the E-Commerce. PayPal is adding millions of new members every day. While eBay has been affected by the downturn in the economy, PayPal is still showing substantial growth. Once you set up a PayPal account you can use it just like a credit card with any seller who is accepting PayPal as a payment method. A payment notification is emailed to you by PayPal.

PayPal is not restricted to eBay. There is a growing number of merchants who are accepting PayPal and including it as a payment option. PayPal offers protection to both buyer and seller. To get PayPal seller protection you must ship only to confirmed or verified addresses. PayPal is linked to your checking account. You can withdraw money or add money to your PayPal account from your checking account and vice versa. One of the great thing you get as a member of PayPal is the ability to print free shipping labels and PayPal is also offering to his sellers members the option to use a tool for prepay shipping to the Postal Service, Canada Post or UPS. In that age of technology and the Internet I can hardly imagine someone living without having a PayPal account. One of the best features that PayPal have now is the fact that PayPal now not only allows shoppers to set up a free account but also they can make online payments via major credit cards, debit cards or electronic checks. This is good news for both online shoppers and online sellers. As a shopper you do not need to be a PayPal member to use this feature. Also, PayPal not only allows you to keep a balance in your PayPal account but also you can earn interest on that balance and you can make purchases using funds from that account. For Online sellers it is very easy to integrate PayPal into their web sites. There are different degrees of integration offered by PayPal depending on the situation of each seller. One of the best features offered for sellers is the fact that if you choose PayPal Pro Service, it will allow you to accept credit cards directly on your web site even if the customer doesn't have a PayPal account. It is the same function as having the traditional credit card merchant account but without the high cost.

Good news for the whole economy is that PayPal has the potential to expand offline. It is bad news for banks and financial institutions but good news for customers and merchants in general.

Chapter 26

Google Checkout

I do not want to leave that book without talking about Google Checkout, which is offered by Google and has emerged recently as a serious competitor to PayPal. Competition is great especially for the seller because the seller is the one who ends up paying the fees. These services are usually free for the online shoppers.

Google is going all the way promoting Google Checkout hoping to replace PayPal. It is offering all kinds of incentives. Their campaign is like this: Buy this service, get that other service for free. Given all the power of Google and the different services it offers, there will be no surprise that Google Checkout will be here to stay. It will be able to at least compete with PayPal head to head if not becoming more popular.

There is a lot of similarity between Google Checkout and PayPal. Google Checkout is free for online shoppers but sellers have to pay fees. For merchants, there is no monthly fee, no set up fee, they only pay fees for each transaction (2% of each sale plus $0.20 per transaction). For merchants, using Google Checkout will help them save a lot of money on their Google AdWords advertising campaign. Yet, they get another benefit. They can use Google Checkout Logo or shopping cart Logo in their online advertising with Google AdWords. Customers will see the logo and gives your ad a lot of attention.

As with PayPal, it is very easy to integrate Google Checkout into your web site. It is another way for merchants to give their customers more options for online payment. For more information about Google Checkout, you can go to the Google web site.

Chapter 27

Making Money by Saving Money

Do you know that a dollar saved is much better than a dollar made. The reason for this is that the dollar you just made, you still have to pay taxes on it but the dollar you saved is considered after tax money. That is why it is worth more. You can use the power of the Internet not just to make money but also to save money. That is what I am doing right now. Everyone can do it. You do not need to have a web site to save money online. You need to have a strategy if you are serious about saving money. If you are going to buy something, check first to see if it is available online and compare prices so you can get the best possible price. Only buy from your local market groceries and heavy objects that can cost a lot in shipping unless the shipping is free. I buy most of the things I need online. One exception is groceries. I believe that local groceries and vegetables are fresh. The first place I go to is usually eBay. There are lots of bargains on eBay. I buy most of my software needs from eBay. There is no doubt that buying from eBay is associated with some risk. To minimize your risk, buy only from merchants with good standing. I only buy from merchants with 500 plus positive feedback. These merchants have been too long on eBay and they will never scam you. The second thing to do to minimize your risk is to pay for your merchandize using PayPal. If anything goes wrong with your transaction, you can get your money back. If you go to the eBay web site, you can find almost everything imaginable for sale on eBay. There are lots of bargains. To be included in this game, you need to sign up for eBay and you need to sign up for PayPal. To get the best bargain on eBay do not put your bid till the last minute and look for merchants that are offering free shipping and no sales tax. I buy my books from half.com. This web site was bought by eBay and now it is part of the eBay company. If you are a member of eBay you can automatically be a member of half.com and you can buy books, CDs and DVDs from this site at a highly discounted price. I usually buy the books I need for almost 70% off. You will save a lot of money if you are a book lover. I buy my computers and laptops from Dell web site. Dell is having an auction site that is selling refurbished computers and laptops among other things. These products are practically new. I bought a lot of computers and laptops from this site at a great price and the merchandize were of high quality. I never had a problem with anything I bought from Dell. Their customer service is great. You can buy a computer for almost have of its retail price. The only problem is that lots of people start to know about that web site and accordingly prices start to go up a little but still a great bargain. You still need to sign up for Dell web site if you want to bid on their products. I also buy from a web site called PropertyRoom.com. This is a real bargain. There are lots of good things over there electronics, computers, coins, tools and other things. I buy tools from that web site. It is practically an auction site and you need to register first before you can use this site. These are most of the good places where I shop online. Always go online and create your own list of your favorite shopping places. In the end you will find yourself saving thousands of dollars. If you can not make money online, you still can save a lot of money.

Chapter 28

Freebies

In this chapter I will talk about three things. I will talk about the free things you can get over the Interne. I will talk about the different kinds of sweepstakes and contests. And finally I will talk about surveys.

There are lots of free stuff you can get over the Internet. All you have to do is just to volunteer some information. Most of the free stuff are offered by companies as promotions or as some sort of advertising. Other marketing companies are going after you're your information especially your email address, your home address and your home phone number. Some of these companies are building up their email lists to use them for email marketing or to sell these email lists to other companies. Your home phone number can be sold to telemarketing companies and your home address can be sold too. I do not want to discourage you from applying to these free stuff. I just need you to be careful. When you apply for free stuff, don't give them your private email or you will be bombarded with email messages. What you need to do is to have a yahoo email to use it in such situations. Also, never volunteer and give them your home phone number and if you do make sure you register with the " Do not call " list or service so that telemarketers can not call you. For me, among the best free things on the Internet, is the free information. It is very valuable. Remember, the Internet is the biggest library in the whole world. You will save a lot of money and time by using these resources. Also, I found the free paying of my bills online is great. I save on the postage and I save money making trips to the Postal Service. Most of the people who apply to the free stuff are the preteen kids who have lots of time on their hands. For me it is not worth the time unless there is something valuable.

Another thing that the Internet is famous for is the thousands of sweepstakes and contests all over the Internet. There is an impression among Internet marketers that in order to attract visitors to your site, you have to offer something for free. You can win cash. You can win trips. You can win electronics, cars and all kinds of stuff. You need to apply same rules I mentioned earlier. Use a Yahoo email and add your home phone number to the " do not call " list. I would like to remind you that anything you win in a contest is taxable. You have to pay taxes on it. To make it even worse, most of the stuff you win in a contest is overvalued especially electronics and trips. So suppose you win a trip to Canada for example, that is values at $10,000.00. It will actually worth $2,000.00 or $3,000.00 for the most, but you end up paying taxes on $10,000.00. When you start doing your taxes at the end of the year, you wish you did not win anything. That is why when I sign up for sweepstakes or contests I make sure the prize is only cash or cars, no overvalued trips.

As for surveys the rewards are different. Some surveys send you some coupons as a thank you gift for filling up their survey. Others pay you a dollar or two a piece. So, if you fill up four surveys an hour, you make at least four dollars. Other surveys put you in a drawing. If you are a winner, you get like $500.00 or even $1,000.00. It is up to you to choose the kind of survey. I found out that surveys are only good for people who have lots of time and have nothing else to do. If you are setting in home for one hour doing nothing, your earning during that hour is practically zero dollars. Otherwise, you can use this time to fill up few surveys and get whatever you can get. It is better than nothing at all.

How you can find out about these opportunities is very easy. Just go to the Google Search Engine and search for free stuff, contests or surveys. You will get thousands of results. By the way you do not need to have your own web site to do these activities. You do not even need to have your own computer or Internet connection. You can just go to any public local library and enjoy free access to the Internet and whatever you want to do.

Chapter 29

Making Money with Online Jobs

There is no doubt that you can use the Internet to look for a full-time or part-time job. There are hundreds of web sites for people looking for employment. You can post your resume for employers to look at. However, this chapter is not meant or dedicated for people looking for full or part-time jobs. This chapter is for people who are looking for work by the job or the project using their special skills. There is nobody in the whole world that doesn't have some kind of a skill. Those who deny having any kind of skills don't know themselves very well. Think about yourself and try to make a list of your skills, the things you can do and make money of it. You will be surprised when you find more than one. Perhaps you can show some people how to do something right e.g. fishing, fixing something, growing some kind of a rare plant and the list goes on. Using the Internet you can sell your skills to the people who need them. You can charge them by the hour or you can charge them by the project. After you make a list of the things you can do design an ad for yourself. You can design an ad like this " I help you learn Microsoft Word 2007 in few hours. Reasonable rates. " or " Can translate from English to French and vice versa. By the project. " and so on. There are lots of sites on the Internet where you can post this ad for free. The most well known site of course is Craig's list. Another well known place is Google base. There are also the free classified offered by Yahoo and Microsoft sites. There are even free local classifieds. If you can do or deliver the work over the Internet you can be everywhere and you can accept work on a global level. If your skills can only get you work locally, you put your ad on the local level. A word of advice is that you need to be careful when dealing with people you do not know. Most of these sites have no control over the ads or who is dealing with who. It is your responsibility to sign and execute the deal. Some web sites have emerged lately and having a lot of controls over deals like this. One of them is Http://www.elance.com. Another one is http://www.clickbank.com. The concepts and ideas in these web sites are almost the same. For example, in elance.com, people who want something done, list their projects and people who have the skills to execute submit their bids and the customer chooses one of the bidders. After you do the work elance.com gets a percentage. The idea of these web sites is so great and can be a great source of income for lots of people that I will discuss both web sites in much more details in separate chapters.

Chapter 30

Making Money with Affiliation Programs

Affiliation programs can be a great source of quick and continuous income if you do it right. You simply make the money by referring customers from your web site to other web site. You can't take advantage of this opportunity unless you have a good working web site with a lot of traffic. If you have a primitive web site with few traffic, forget about this opportunity. Your web site should look professional at least, because some of the merchants offering these affiliate programs want to have a look at your web site first before they approve you for their program. You should use every means to promote your web site and attract more visitors because without traffic, you can't make any money. The advantage of affiliate programs is that you are practically not selling anything. You do not have to worry about inventory or shipping. You do not need to have a shopping cart, a payment system or even a merchant account. Your web site can be very simple.

There are thousands of affiliate programs online. There is almost an affiliate program for every product or service. When you sign up for a merchant's affiliate program you will be given a link to post in your web site. Visitors to your web site click on that link and this action will take them to the merchant's web site. Some programs pay you just for this action. Other programs will pay you only if your customer takes some action like signing up for something. Still other programs will not pay you unless they make a sale and this is the most rewording. The best way to achieve success is through providing good articles and at the end of each article you make your recommendations and provide the link. For example, if you have a good article about solar energy, your article should be very impressive. At the end of the article you mention your recommendations concerning the best companies that are offering solar products or services, the best books about solar and so on. Your credibility goes hand in hand with how good your article is. If you provide an excellent article, your customers will believe your recommendations. Free articles are a great way to attract more traffic to your web site.

A good advice is to sign only for good merchants; those who you believe are providing good service or high quality product at a reasonable price. You do not want your audience to lose confidence in you. If you deceive your customers they will never come back to you. So, my best advice to you is to choose your affiliate programs very carefully. Don't recommend a service or a product to someone unless they are excellent. I do not just go and recommend something because they are going to pay me a good commission. In the short run you will win but in the end you will lose. As I said before, there are thousands of affiliate programs and you have a great opportunity to pick and choose. Before you sign up for an affiliate program go to the merchant's web site and check everything. Your impression about the merchant's web site in general, the customer service, the products offered etc. It is your reputation that will be on the line.

You should specialize in one thing e.g. photography, electronics, web hosting, money etc. Then try to get some articles about that field you are in. If you don't know how to write good articles, hire someone to do the job for you. Check out the leaders in that field and find out if they provide affiliate programs. Sign up with the best of them. If you try to sign up for everybody and you just providing a web site that has nothing but a group of links, your chance of success is very small. You will get no traffic because search engines will not rank you very well. Even if you get some traffic your customers will not believe you or believe your recommendations. Your credibility will be at minimal.

The widespread of affiliate programs has led to the creation of what is called affiliate networks. Affiliate networks have a database of thousands of affiliate programs that you can browse and sign up for as many as you like. You need to sign up for the affiliate network first and you need to be approved. Some of them approve you immediately, others take some time to approve you. It doesn't cost you any money to apply for these affiliate networks. The affiliate network pays your commission in the form of a one monthly paycheck regardless of how many affiliate programs you sign up for. One of the best known affiliate networks is the construction Junction at http://www.CJ.Com. There are many others. You can find out about them by doing a search on Google.Com for affiliate networks.

Before you commit yourself you need to collect as much information as you can about affiliate programs so you can do it right. You can make thousands of dollars each month if you do the right thing. It only takes a lot of work in the beginning but once it is set up you only have to set down and watch the money coming.

Chapter 31

Making Money with Unclaimed Property

Do you know that the States hold billions of dollars in unclaimed assets. There are all kinds of property. The source of this property is the fact that people pass away leaving all kinds of property that their heirs don't know anything about. Old paychecks, utility refunds, stocks, bank accounts, contents of safe deposit boxes and life insurance policies, just to name a few. In Pennsylvania State alone, the unclaimed property division of PA treasury Department holds more than $1.6 billion in unclaimed assets. It is estimated that more than one quarter of all life insurance benefits go unclaimed because family members are not aware that the policy exists. The issue of unclaimed life insurance is a big one. It is probably more common than most people think. Most people who purchase a life insurance policy feel they have taken the first step in protecting their family. But they don't realize the fact that life insurance companies have no way of knowing when a policy holder passes away. It is expected that unclaimed life insurance will become more common as people live longer. Some people may have a policy that they are no longer paying premiums on it, so they throw it in a drawer and forget about it. When a company owes money to someone but can't find that person or when a bank account lies untouched for 3 years and the owner can't be reached, the funds must be turned over to the state's unclaimed property division. The cash stays with the government unless a claim is made by the owner or the heirs. In the State of Pennsylvania, it is estimated that about one in ten Pennsylvanians has unclaimed property. All the unclaimed property is held in the general fund until it is claimed. Until then, it continues to earn interest for the owners. There is no time limit on claiming the property. The problem is that the states don't make any effort to locate these people or their heirs and if they do, it is a modest effort. This lack of effort by the states can create an opportunity for you to find these people and make some money by charging them a finder fee. You can just work in your state or you can work all over the country. The Internet is your friend that will make your job easy. Almost every state has a web site for the unclaimed assets in that state. For example if you intend to do that work in Pennsylvania State, you can search the State's unclaimed property records database at http://www.patreasury.org. You can do a free online search for unclaimed assets through the National Association of

Unclaimed Property Administrators web site at http://www.MissingMoney.Com; a database of governmental unclaimed property records.

The next step is to find these people. How you can find them is through your best friend; the online search engines. Suppose you find a person who has unclaimed property somewhere, the first call is very critical. If that person hangs up on you, don't give up. You need to excuse people if they hang up on you, because there are all kinds of scams out there. You need to choose your words very carefully. Introduce yourself first and talk in a very friendly manner. When you call that person, don't tell him the whole story. If you tell him or her everything, there will be no need of you anymore. Just tell them that there is money waiting for them and you need a finder fee to help them cash in. Tell them that you going to tell them all the details after you sign a contract with them to preserve your right. Your fee should not be more than a 10%.

You don't need a web site to do all of this. All you need is a computer that is connected to the Internet.

Chapter 32

A Web Site for A Non-Profit

Have you ever thought about having your own nonprofit organization?! There are thousands of nonprofit organizations all over the country and in the whole World. There are so many of the nonprofit organizations that there is a directory for them in the Internet. People create nonprofits for all kinds of motives. Some people believe that their nonprofit is going to change the world for better. Some people can't find a job, so they create a job for themselves by creating a nonprofit organization. This way they can have a job, salary and the benefit of helping other people.

The Internet has revolutionized the way nonprofits are doing business. Setting up a web site has helped nonprofits cut costs dramatically, raises more money and do their jobs in a more efficient way. Almost anyone can start a nonprofit. All you have to do is to have an idea that appeals to the public because that is where your income will be coming from. Follow all the rules and the laws for establishing a nonprofit. Your organization has to be legally allowed to raise money. There is a lot of information on the Internet about how to establish a nonprofit, how to run it, how to raise money and the legal aspects of a nonprofit organization. You can go to your local library and borrow some books about the subject.

The web site for a nonprofit is very simple, easy to setup and straightforward. You can create a web site for a nonprofit in minutes. Most likely, your web site hosting company has a template to build up a web site for a nonprofit organization. Your mission should be clearly posted in a prominent part of the main page. Since you are going to raise most of the money with the help of your web site, you need to fully describe what your organization is going to do and why people should donate money to your organization. Make it easy for your audience to donate by having the ability to accept credit cards, checks and other forms of payment. You can integrate PayPal payment system in your web site. It is free and can help you accept credit card payments with a minimal cost. You can even sell other items that are related to the cause you are adopting e.g. T-shirts, mugs and other things. There should be a contact page with the email and phone number of the organization. Also, I encourage you to include an inquiry form. A good customer service is a must. A good marketing plan is critical to the survival of your organization. It can make or break it. You should have a plan for fund raising and follow the rules. This is so critical that if you can't do it yourself, you can hire someone else to do it for you. There are some companies specialized in fund raising but they take at least 3% of the money they raise. If you can live with this, you can go this way.

Another source of income for your organization is to accept advertising like the most popular Google AdSense. You need to be creative and have great content to convince people to donate.

Visit some of these nonprofit web sites to look at the design, how they appeal to the public, how they raise funds and how they present the information. Look at the content and the general layout. Copy their success.

Chapter 33

Directory of Import Export Web Site

We are living in the age of global economy. Foreign trading is at its maximum. Everyone is trying to benefit from globalization. You should do the same thing. You can create a web site that is offering information about that topic to your audience. Your information is nothing more than a detailed directory about companies in the US that are engaged in the import export business. You need to organize them in categories. To have the competitive edge over other web sites that are offering the same service, you can rate these companies according to specific criteria like type of the products, customer service and your final recommendations. Those companies that are given good rating and good recommendations can be your target to join their affiliate programs. This can be a very good source of income for you. I already discussed affiliated programs in a previous chapter. You can go back and read it. Another source of income for you is the fact that you can accept Google AdSense advertising. Your web site design will be straight forward. You do not need a shopping cart or a payment processing system. All you need is a good content. Make sure to include detailed information about companies in your directory. Visit other web sites that are doing the same thing and ask yourself this question: How can I be better than them ?. Your costs should be minimal. You only have to pay for web hosting which can be between $10 and $20 a month. You can use a template from your web hosting company. All you have to do is to fill it up with good content. So far you will be having two sources of income; affiliate programs and advertising. The amount of money you will be making depends on you and how much traffic you are getting. This is the kind of web site that can make you money while you are asleep. Just set it up and forget it. You only need to update the information once in a while.

Another good source of income is to establish yourself as an expert in the import export business. This means people and companies from other countries can consult you about doing business with companies in the U.S. You can do this for a fee. Project yourself as professional as you can and make your fees negotiable. The Internet can be a great asset for you to collect the information that your customers are looking for.

Do not limit yourself to sources of income I just mentioned. You can always explore other income avenues.

Chapter 34

Doing Business Somewhere Web Site

We talked before about the global economy and how people are trying to find and discover new markets. This is your chance to make some money with this opportunity. All you have to do is to gather some information, categorize it in an easy to read manner and post them in your web site. As I said before, in a global economy, people are always looking for new markets. Some people want to do business in China; others want to do business in India; still others in Egypt and so on. These people are on the look for information. They need as much information as they get about their specific target country. There are more than 100 countries all over the World. Each one of these countries is considered a unique market with unique laws, unique habits and customs, unique population, unique geography and unique economy. How about targeting only one of these markets! Gather as much information as you can about it. Organize that information and present it in an easy to read manner in your web site. Your web site should be the best source of information about that specific country. It will take a lot of work to be at the top. Once you are at the top your chance of making real money will be excellent. The way you present this important data is critical to your success. Suppose you choose a country like China. I start by collecting all the information about China with great emphasis on the information that is essential to business people. Everything matters. Talk about how you can travel to China. Mention the advantages of doing business in China. Language and education in China should be mentioned. Also, I talk about the Chinese people, what they like and dislike, their customs and their habits, their hobbies and manners. Also, I talk about things that can offend the Chinese people and things that make them happy. Most important is to talk about trade laws, shipping, tariffs, taxes, business laws, best places to do business there, best places to visit, etc. Also very important is to talk about the infrastructure, the road system and the telecommunications. Most important are the available investment opportunities, the markets and the directory of the Chinese companies that have global activities. You collect all the information that is important to anyone who is willing to do business in that country and present that information in a well designed, well organized manner in your web site. I do not recommend choosing big countries with big economies like China or India because you will have a lot of competition. Go for small developing countries that are looking for investors. These countries will be very happy to provide you with a lot of information. It will be a good idea to select the country where you, your parents or grandparents came from because, most of the time, you will be familiar with it. If you feel you can have the competitive advantage, you can go ahead and choose China, India, Japan or whatever country you like.

You can make money from this web site by accepting advertising and also you can offer consulting for a nominal fee. You can offer your consulting service in the form of a report that you can send by email, so it will not cost you a dime.

Your web site should not cost you more than the monthly fee of the web hosting company. Even the hosting company should have templates that you can use and you just add the contents and you are done.

Chapter 35

Outsourcing Web Site

We all know what outsourcing is. The fact is that not everybody agrees whether it is good or bad for the economy and the whole country in general. Outsourcing is happening everyday and no one will be able to stop or change this trend. In my opinion, outsourcing can sometimes be bad for the economy and, in some situations, it can be good to the country. Outsourcing is considered bad to the country when a company moves a whole factory or department overseas. It is like taking a piece of the American economy away. On the other hand, outsourcing is considered good when you bring a talented individual from overseas to this country. This talented individual will enrich the economy and participate in the community here including the spending part. Generally, in a situation like this, the overall effect is positive.

With your web site, you will do the good side of outsourcing which is bringing talented people here. This is how it works. Talented people from overseas will come to your web site and write down their profile, post their resume, photo, skills and credentials and what they are looking for. This should be done at no cost to them. These individual data will be kept in a database. Companies which are looking for talented people from overseas will come to your site. They can pay a membership fee or they can pay per visit to check out that database. If they find someone that are interested in, they can contact that individual directly or they can ask for your help. You can act as a mediator between the talented person and the company. There will be a contract to be signed, papers to be filed to bring that person legally into the country, travel, accommodations and other things. You can offer all these services and more for a fee. The company can contract with you and pay you for these services. A lot of companies do not have the human resources to handle all that paper work. Your web site doesn't need to be highly sophisticated. You do need to connect to a database program like Microsoft SQL or MySQL. Most of the web hosting companies have a database program that you can connect to. Probably you will need a lot of help and technical support to do it right. Also you need to post a lot of articles and information about the good side of outsourcing. You need to stress the fact that the part of outsourcing you are doing is not taking away American jobs. Generally the people in this country do not like the concept of outsourcing at all.

You also need to have a separate page in which you explain the different services that are offered by your web site. Email marketing is very important for you to survive. You need to inform the American companies that you are here and available to help them. Tell them about your services and how you are going to make their lives easier. You need to email the good educational institutions in countries where there are lots of talents e.g. India and China. You need to use the power of the social networking sites and video sharing sites to spread the word. You need to have a presence in all of these sites.

Your source of income from a web site like this will be the membership fees and the fees you charge for the other services you are offering. You can also make some money of advertising. You can include PayPal and Google Checkout in your web site as your payment methods at the beginning. In the future, you can include more payment options.

Chapter 36

Best of the Best Directory Web Site

This web site is one of the easiest to build when it comes to design and cost. At the same time, it could be a good money maker if you design it right and post the right information in it. In our normal daily life, people are usually buying things, applying for something and doing other activities. There are lots of retail places with millions of different products, lots of services and consumers are confused. There is always this question: Which is the best?. Customers want a good product or service with a reasonable price. This is where you are going to help them. You will do a lot of research to find out the best places to buy different products and services with high quality at a great price. For example, if I am looking for auto insurance, I go to your web site to find out the best company offering that service and so on. A lot of this information is already in the web but it is scattered everywhere. Your best source of information is the Consumer Reports Web Site, but the problem is that they do not have a report about everything. Here is your job to fill up the gap. For your web site to look professional, you need to have categories; a lot of categories and subcategories. Include a lot of categories like eBay, and always add more categories for more products and services. Each category should have subcategories. Start with each subcategory and make a list of the companies which are offering that product or that service. Make a rating system from scale one to ten to rate these companies. State the best thing about each company. Your rating system should depend on three factor: quality of the product, the price and the customer service. For each product or service list at least five companies with details about what is so good about each of them. In the end, your directory should contain thousands of companies. People who are looking for a product or service will come to your web site first to check out who the best is. You need to generate a lot of trust. People who use your site should be allowed to leave a feedback about their shopping experience. Bad companies should be removed of your list immediately. You need to pay a lot of attention to the details and your categories should practically cover everything. You need to provide a search engine on your site since your site will be so big. This search engine tool can be provided by Google. It is very easy to integrate it into your site and very easy to use.

Make your customer participate. If anyone knows about a good company give them the chance to mention it. You can check it out then include it in your system.

Your big source of income in this case is to affiliate with most of these companies and earn a commission each time you send them a customer. Another source of income will be Google Adsense. You can accept ads on your site.

Your cost will be minimal in this case. You do not need a payment processing system or a shopping cart. You just pay a monthly hosting fee. But you need to keep updating your list on a regular basis because there are always new companies every day. Your customers can be a great source of information for you. Their feedback will be very important and you should take it seriously.

A very important point that can make or break your business in the long run is the level of trust among your customers. A lot of companies are offering big commission and at the same time, offering bad service or bad product. You should not be fooled by that big commission. Never include a company based on the amount of commission. It will only take few customers to destroy your business.

Chapter 37

Making Money Web Site

Ask everybody about his first wish. Most people will tell you that their first wish is to make more money. Everybody wants to make more money. People are always on the look for ways to boost their income and get rich. Even the rich people want to be richer. Your target audience should be the people who don't make enough money and have the desire to make more. Your job is to help them by offering real good opportunities. There are thousands of web sites that promise you to make money and get rich. There are thousands of books about making money. Most of these resources don't offer what they promise and there are lots of scams involved. People are getting burned every day. They spend a lot of money, effort and time but they end up with nothing. There are very few real opportunities out there. Your job is to identify these good real opportunities and present them to your customers. You need to be honest and offers only the ideas that you think are going to work. A lot of money web sites endorse some programs about making money. Do not do that. This will do more harm to you in the long run. You have to make it clear that your site is independent and you do not accept any money from anybody and you are not endorsing any program or idea. This will generate a lot of trust among your audience and they will keep coming back to look for new ideas. Put a lot of stress on hard work. There is nothing called easy money. If there is, we all will be rich. You have to work hard and smart to make it. Do not make false or exaggerated claims like make thousands of dollars doing this and that. People know from experience that these claims are bogus and you can't prove it. Instead of saying make thousands of dollars, say make a decent income or make additional income or make some more money and so on. This way will make people believe you.

This web site model is better be done as a blog. This way you can let your customers participate and discuss your claims and you will get a lot of feedback. This will enrich your site and will keep it updated on a regular basis. Search engines love this. You can get a high ranking among different search engines.

When you have an idea that you think people can make money with it, just post it and ask your visitors about their opinions. Ask them to discuss the topic honestly. Ask them to post any ideas they think it could help people like you and me make more money. There are lots of ideas for this kind of a web site.

You can't make money from this web site by affiliating with any other programs. It will generate a lot of mistrust and turn your audience away. People are already having a lot of mistrust dealing with this issue in general. So try to be honest, serious and clear. The only way to make money with this site is to accept advertising ads like Google AdSense. If you succeed and generate a lot of audience you could make a lot of money from advertising.

In addition to discussing ways to make money, you need to post some articles to protect your audience from losing money to scams. Teaching your audience about how to spot a scam from a real money making opportunity is great. You can also teach your customers how to fight back should they lose some money to a con artist. There are lots of other good topics that are related to money and you can package them and present them to your visitors in the form of good useful articles.

Chapter 38

Saving Money Web Site

This is the other side of the coin. People not only like to make money but they also like to save money at the same time. Saving money is the second part of the game. Actually, a dollar saved is better than a dollar made because the dollar you save is considered after tax money; you already paid tax on it but the dollar you just made you still have to pay tax on it. This is another good opportunity for you to help other people and help yourself by making some money out of that web site. How about having a web site that is filled up with tips and serious recommendations for saving money?. It is very easy to collect all that information. Just try to pick up the stuff that makes sense. People don't have time to read about lots of things that don't work or save them just few pennies. Make sure that the information you collect is practical, easy to follow and easy to apply. Also, make sure it is going to work. Your site should be very organized and easy to navigate. This can be done by including your information in categories like saving money on autos, saving money on food and so on. At the same time you can make your own recommendations about certain companies or businesses. This will help you making affiliations with these companies and get some sort of revenue for the site. At the same time your recommendations should be honest and based on solid facts. It doesn't hurt to recommend a certain good insurance company or a certain web hosting company but you have to make sure that they are good and your customers will save money by dealing with them. If you misled your visitors, they will never come back to your site again. You have to spend some effort to make sure that this company or business will actually save money to your audience.

Tell your audience about the value of using grocery coupons and how to use them right. There are hundreds of good tips to save money and in this kind of economy people are serious about saving money. If they can't make more money, they still can save some money and live within their means.

Again, this web site is better be designed as a blog, so you can ask your audience to contribute. A lot of people have great ideas about saving money and they are willing to share these ideas with other people. A blog will be your chance to build a community that shares one goal. This one goal is to save money.

I expect you to make a lot of money with this web site if you do it right and if you post a high quality content. This is a very serious subject especially these days. To make money with this site you can accept advertising especially the Google AdSense. Also you can join affiliate programs. For every company that you recommend to your audience, you can affiliate with that company. If you are looking for more revenue, you can offer some products or services for sale. You need to make sure that these products and services are good bargains and your audience is going to save money by buying from your site. In this case, you will need a shopping cart and some sort of payment processing system. This will add to your basic cost of doing business. But if you think it is going to bring you additional revenue, it is a good idea to include them. Do not forget to always ask for more feedback from your customers and to update the content of your web site or blog on a regular basis. A good content is your biggest asset.

Chapter 39

How To Web Site

Do you know that most of the people go to the Internet to look for information. You can capitalize on this by having a web site that teaches people how to do something. There are lots of how to web sites on the Internet. If you are going to copy them you will be out of luck when it comes to making money with your web site. You have to compete with all of them and your job will be hard to impossible. You need to do it the way I recommend it. Of course, you have heard about the term branding. This is what you need to do. You need to be specialized in a very tiny topic and try to make everybody an expert in that topic. I give you an example. If you are going to teach people about home improvement, this is going to be a very broad topic. You will have a lot of competition, you will not be able to present a lot of details and in the end, you will not be able to build a community because you do not have a brand. Instead, make a list of home improvement projects and just pick up that one you think it will have an audience e.g. building a fancy fireplace, building a fancy swimming pool and so on. Once you pick up a brand or topic, go deep into it. Offer your audience all kinds of details. You are supposed to be an expert in this tiny subject, so your visitors will be expecting too much from your web site. This way you can build your own community. Even if your topic is so narrow, you will have a lot of users. This will surprise you. Do not underestimate the global nature of the Internet. Your web site can be seen by millions and millions of people around the globe. Your success will depend on a lot of things. The first thing is the subject or topic of your web site. There are topics that have a lot of appeal like health and money. The second thing is how crazy your audience is about the chosen topic. The third thing is the quality of the content of your web site. There is no way for you to succeed if you pick up a topic that people do not care about. There are lots of ways to check what people are searching the web for. Start with this and then you can go from there. There is no way to succeed if the content of your site is not informative enough and doesn't satisfy your audience. Your web site content should not only be of value but also be updated on a regular basis.

You can make money from your web site in several ways. Since you are an expert on the subject of your web site, you can sell your skills to your audience. A second source of revenue is to accept ads in your web site like Google AdSense. A third way to make money with this web site is through affiliation programs. There are companies you are going to recommend for your audience to do business with. You can affiliate with these companies. A last source of revenue from your web site is to start selling products that are related to the topic of your web site. People will be willing to buy from you because you build up trust.

How to web sites are not hard to build or design. Choosing the right topic is a good start. Usually your web hosting company has a template for building a how to web site. This will make your job easy. You have to take advantage of that. You only need to modify it and integrate the Ecommerce tools so you can sell the products and services to your visitors.

Chapter 40

Business Start Ups Web Site

There are thousands of people trying to start new businesses every day. It is everybody's dream to have his own business one day especially in this country. It is not easy, however, to start a new business especially if you have never had a business before. There are lots of issues that needed to be addressed. This is your chance to help start ups with your web site. You need to inform them about the legal issues of starting a business, how to make a business plan, how to apply for capital or grants, how to build a web site for your business, how to hire employees and many other issues. If you intend to present all the issues and details of starting a new business, your web site will be huge but the rewards will be big too.

The good thing about setting up a site like this is the fact that although you will have to spend a lot of time at the beginning collecting all that information and posting it to your web site, your efforts after this will be minimal. Once you have your web site up and running, you do not need to spend a lot of time to maintain it because most of its content is static. You only need to update when you find something new or something missing.

There are many ways to make money with a web site like this. You can work as a consultant to start ups. You can make money consulting, giving lectures and seminars. Even you can give courses in community colleges. Another source of revenue is advertising. You can make a lot of money with Google AdSense. It is easy to apply for and easy to integrate into your web site. A third source of income is from affiliation programs. As you post all that information to start ups in your web site, you can recommend a lot of good resources, services and products to your audience. You need to provide them, at the same time, with a sense of honesty and trust. You need to show them that that your primary goal is to help them get started. If they trust you, they will take your recommendations for granted and click the links you provide to go to the sites that you are recommending. Every company of these has an affiliate program. You can affiliate with all these sites to provide you with another source of income.

You need to be aware of the fact that there is a lot of competition in that field. So you need to have what they call the competitive advantage. This can be in the form of high quality content, good customer service or easy to navigate web site.

I do not recommend selling any products or services on this web site because it is already big enough. You can only sell your expertise to whoever asks for it.

If your web site has everything that a start up needs, your audience will keep coming back. As you get more traffic, different search engines will give a high ranking. So, if you intend to get into that field, you need to start right by posting everything a start up needs, so they do not have to go to someplace else to look for more information. At the same time, people do not like wasting their time looking at useless information. Your information should add a value and makes a difference.

Chapter 41

A Web Site For Health Issues

There is no doubt that everybody on the surface of the earth is worried about his health. A lot of people are actively trying to be well educated about certain medical issues. Some people are concerned about diabetes. Others are concerned about their weight. Some are concerned about heart issues. Others want to live a long healthy life and so on. You can set up a web site dealing with one of these health issues. There are thousands of web sites dealing with health issues. You can't stand a chance competing with them. They have a lot of resources much more than you do. But they are like a medical encyclopedia. If you try to be like them; a medical encyclopedia, you will fail miserably. Your best approach is to pick up only one subject or topic you feel that it will have a lot of audience. Pick up a topic that people care about. Pick up something like alcoholism, adult diabetes, weight loss etc. Even these topics are still broad in the Internet world. You will be better off if you try to narrow your topic as much as you can.

After you pick up your favorite subject, your next step is to collect all the relevant information about that subject. Present that information in an easy to read manner. Divide that information into a lot of topics. Give as much details as you can. Give your recommendations concerning services and products. If there are products that can be sold on your web site, make a list of them and offer them for sale to your audience. These products and services should be directly related to the topic of your web site.

Remember that you are trying to set up a web site to be a reference for that topic. This will help you build a loyal community that keeps coming back to your web site for more.

This kind of a web site is very simple to set up. Your web hosting company may have a template to help you with the set up process. If you are going to sell in big volume, you will need a shopping cart and a payment processing system. You can make money with this web site in many ways. Selling products and services can be one source of revenue. Joining some affiliate programs can be another source of revenue. A third source of revenue is to accept advertising like Google AdSense. You need to offer a great customer service and to answer questions and inquiries as soon as you get them. Also you need to regularly update your web site because there is always something new when it comes to health issues.

I can suggest to you some of the subjects or topic that can work fine for this web site.

Live stress free life.

Painless weight loss.

What can you do for children with diabetes.

Adult diabetes and good life style.

The aging process and how you can live a healthy long life.

Coping with a disability.

Young forever; way to look and feel younger.

Nursing homes; a solution or part of a problem.

Smoking.

The forgotten; how you can cope with living alone.

How you can overcome sleepless nights.

Dreams; do they mean anything?!

Natural healings.

How you can overcome general fatigue.

Autistic child in the family!

And much more.

Chapter 42

Go Wireless Web Site

It is the wireless revolution. You can feel it everywhere; your phone, your computer, your electricity and the list is growing by the day. Everyone is happy about it. No missy cables on the floor anymore and you have more freedom to move. There are some security issues but they are working on these issues to make the wireless revolution more secure. This is the topic of your web site. You can discuss everything that is wireless. Educate your customers about the wireless revolution. What is wireless? How does it work? What are the available wireless products? Who are the leaders in that field? Is wireless the way to go? Is it safe?

A lot of issues you can explain to your customers. This will give you the competitive advantage over your competitors. It will take a lot of work to set up a web site like this but the reward can be very great. This topic is very important to everybody. You will build a very huge audience who will help you make a lot of money.

First, you need to include wireless tutorials in the form of articles and how to e.g. how to set up a wireless home network. Include as many articles as you can. Then you need to include categories of different wireless products and the name of the top producers of each product. Include a link to each one of them. You need to educate your customers about the exact use of each of these products.

You need to include in your web site a shopping store where people can buy their wireless needs directly from your site. If you can do it right, you can beat all your competitors because people need the right information before making a decision to buy and you will provide them with the right information and the right product at the same time in just one stop. Your revenue from a web site like this can skyrocket. You will be having a lot of advertising thanks to all that traffic that you will be getting. You can affiliate with every company that you have a link to in your web site. This can be a great source of income to you. At the same time, your store will be open 24 hours a day, 7 days a week.

With this kind of a web site, a good customer service is a must. In most cases, if things go right you will not be able to handle everything by yourself. You will need to hire more qualified people.

Despite all that rosy picture that I just gave you, I still feel that the topic is too broad to handle in just one web site. A better way is to just specialize in one topic of the wireless world. For example, your web site can be dedicated only to the subject of security of the wireless networks or wireless home networking. You can even sell kits for wireless home networking or kits to build WiFi networks for small businesses. You can even just specialize in wireless routers. You can only specialize in wireless antenna. In my opinion, it is better to deal in a small area in the wireless world than dealing with the whole subject of wireless. You still will get a lot of loyal audience and you will get higher ranking among different search engines.

Chapter 43

Search Engine Optimization Web Site

If you need your web site to be seen, you need to register with as many search engines as you can. This is how web sites are viewed on the Internet. Suppose you are looking for something on the Internet, the usual thing that most of the people do is to go to a search engine web site, mostly Google, Yahoo or Microsoft, and write few words about what they are looking for. The search engine immediately provides them with the search results in the form of a very long list of web sites that probably have the information they are looking for. Most people do not go over the whole list. Instead, they usually review the first few sites at the top of the list. So if your web site is not listed in the first page i.e. a high rank, your chance of being seen is close to nothing. That is why every web site owner is fighting for a high rank. And that is why a new business called search engine optimization has come to life. These companies that are engaged in search engine optimization claim to help you achieve a high rank but there is no guarantee, since everybody is fighting for the same thing. I do not want you to start a business similar to these companies because probably you do not have the expertise and you will run into problems with your customers because as I said before there is no guarantee that the web site of your customer will achieve a high rank despite doing all the necessary changes and modifications. Even if you manage to get a high rank to your customer, it will not last for too long.

What I want you to do is very simple. Start a web site that educate people about what to do to achieve a high ranking. You need to read a lot of references about the subject. You need to research the Internet for any useful material about that topic. Collect a lot of information and write down that information in easy to understand steps. Whenever you find out about something new, just go and update your web site. A good thing about adopting this topic is that you can apply what you learn on your own web site to optimize it first. So you can have a proof of what really works.

You can only money with this kind of a web site by advertising. I do not recommend that you affiliate with any of these companies that do search engine optimization because most of the time they have dissatisfied customers which will be reflected on you. You can make some more money by using your expertise in the field. You can teach, consult, give seminars but do not promise people of anything. You need to tell them that search engine optimization is a long and continual process. You have to explain this to your audience. They have to work hard for the life of their web site to achieve a high ranking. It is not a one time process and you are done.

This web site idea can be better done in the form of a blog. This way your customers can interact and leave comments on the subject. A lot of people have valuable information and they are more than willing to share that information with other people. By having a blog , you are going to enrich your site and make it more valuable.

Chapter 44

Digital Photography Web Site

Digital photography is a very popular topic. If you want to know how popular digital photography is, just look at how many digital cameras are sold every year. Everybody is cashing in and so should you. There are lots of web sites and blogs talking about the subject but still there is more room for new comers. Before you do anything, go and visit these web sites and blogs to get an idea about that market. Ask yourself what you can do more to have the competitive advantage. Your web site should show a lot of articles about photography and types of digital cameras available in the market. Also you should include a lot of articles about using the right product for the right job.

The subject of photography is actually too broad that you can divide it into pieces and pick up just one piece. If you specialize in just one topic of photography, you might do better. For example, you can discuss only digital cameras or video camcorders and so on. It is up to you. If you have a lot of resources you can handle the whole subject of photography.

You can recommend certain products and items to your audience. You can also offer different products for sale in your web site.

Your web site should be easy to navigate and download fast. If you are going to sell products make sure you post very good pictures of these products, showing all the details. Remember that your customers are away from you. They can't feel or touch the product you are offering for sale, so you better show them good pictures. Mention what the product is capable of doing and what the product can't do. If you recommend a certain brand be honest. You recommend that brand because you feel it will do the job right not because you are affiliating with the product company and the company pay you a commission to market the product. You are trying to build up a community around your web site. Your articles and free courses should be very easy to understand with a lot of good information. People do not have time to waste.

If you do your job right, you can make a lot of money with this web site. If you can't do it all yourself, hire some help. You can make money with this web site in a variety of ways. If you manage to attract a lot of traffic, people will look at you as an expert in the field. You can capitalize on this by offering lectures, courses, seminars, speeches and even consulting. All of these activities are not going to be free. You can also accept advertising in your web site. Another source of revenue is the merchandise you are selling. Also, you can join affiliation programs where you can affiliate with the companies that you are recommending in your web site. It will take a lot of work and a lot of patience to be at the top of the game.

Chapter 45

IVF Web Site

IVF stands for In vitro fertilization. This is an advanced technique used by some clinics to help couples have kids. These couples usually can't have kids the normal way. This is usually done for women who don't have eggs. So, the doctors arrange for what is called egg donors. The egg donor should be young, able to produce eggs and have good genes. Some people for example, want the egg donor to be very pretty so they can have pretty off springs. Others require the egg donors to be very smart, so they can have very smart kids and so on. The egg donor gets paid usually thousands of dollars to donate her eggs.

In some case, the woman who wants to have kids is not even capable of carrying a baby. In this case, she needs more help. She needs another female to carry the baby for her. This is called a surrogate mother. The doctor will put the fertilized egg in her womb and she carries the baby. After delivery, the family which initiates the whole process gets the baby. The surrogate mother gets paid too, usually thousands of dollars.

There are lots of money to be made in this business. What you can do is to offer these services to the medical doctors and the public in general. You can start a web site that brings those who need donors and or surrogates with the females who want to volunteer.

You can get a lot of volunteers by explaining to them that what they are doing is going to help other families. Anyone who wants to an egg donor or a surrogate mother can have a personal profile in your web site for free. The prospective volunteer can fill up a form, download some pictures and provides her personal information and her contact email. Anyone who is looking for an egg donor or a surrogate can access your database for a fee. They can pay a membership fee which is good for medical doctors in the field or they can pay a certain amount of money each time they try to access your web site. You can do it anyway you like. I prefer that each person who wants to access your database to pay $50.00 each time and it is up to them to contact the volunteers. You need to advertise your services to the women clinics and specially fertility clinics.

I do not believe you will have a lot of competition but if you succeed, probably a lot of people will try to copy your success. You need, of course, to add a lot of information about the whole process. Also, you need to explain to your audience what your web site is all about. It is a good idea to accept volunteers from all over the world, so you can increase your base. You can modify your web site to accept advertising that is related to women health. Also, you can sell products that are related to the topic and to women health in general. If you plan and design that web site right you can make a lot of money. You will have a high ranking among search engines and you can get a lot of traffic.

A word of caution is not to try to expand your business by trying to get yourself involved in the arrangements or contracts between donors and recipients. There are lots of legal issues associated with this and you do not want to get into trouble. Make it clear that you do not sponsor or recommend any of the volunteers. There is no way to verify the accuracy of the information posted by the volunteers. It is up to the recipients to verify everything before contracting with any of these volunteers. This statement should be enough to get you out of any legal trouble should any problem arises.

Chapter 46

Video Conference Web Site

Video conference technology allows two or more people in different locations to sit next to each other and have a conversation. This business is growing real fast. In 2008, the global video conferencing market was $2.4 billion. It is estimated that this market will be more than double by the year 2013 to reach $5.7 billion. Businesses now of all sizes, have to cut on business travel because of the current economic conditions. They realized that the technology of video conferencing available now can save them thousands of dollars. You can save on airfares, hotels, restaurants etc. A very important thing is that you can save on time. Also, video conference systems and equipment are more affordable and more reliable than ever these days. There are systems in the market now designed for small businesses that sell for less than $10,000.00 dollar. Also, Internet bandwidth is plentiful and affordable. This business is the fastest growing business ever. You need to get into that game as soon as you can.

Before you start working on your web site, you need to grasp the subject of video conferencing very well. Gather as much details as you can. You need to know the large video conferencing equipment suppliers. Cisco is a big one and considered a leader in this field. Others are the California based Polycom and Tandberg. You need to know the different systems that are offered by each of these companies. Your target will be small businesses. You can sell whole systems. You can also install, educate and maintain these systems. For each system you are selling, try to design a video demo for it so your customers can have an idea about what they are getting. As a marketing tool, you need to stress the savings that these businesses will realize by installing these systems. You need to explain in your web site how video conferencing technology works. What the expectations are. Video conferencing technology is great for companies that have lots of branches in the US or all over the World.

You will have multiple sources of revenue. You can accept ads in your web site. You are going to make money selling real solutions to companies and businesses. You can also sell your skills and expertise in the field of video conferencing. You can also sign up for the affiliation programs offered by the companies that dealing with video conferencing equipment and services.

Chapter 47

Kits to Go Web Site

What is a kit? It is simply a plan for a small project. For example, there is a small kit to build a swimming pool, another kit to make something for a child to play with and so on. There are thousands of kits that are designed to help people and make their lives easier. People are more than happy to buy them. I found someone on the Internet selling a kit about to build a wireless home network. Another one is selling a kit about how to make fuel from used vegetable oils. You can design your own kits and sell it on the Internet. You can find ideas everywhere on the web. You will never run out of ideas. A good place to find ideas is http://www.ehow.com. Another great place is http://www.YouTube.com. These are just two best places. There are hundreds more over there. Once you have an idea, start building on that idea and develop a kit for people. That kit must be easy to apply and will add a value to the user. Your kit should have the ability to make a difference or people will never buy it. Before you design your web site you need to make a choice on the way to proceed. You can concentrate your effort on just one topic and build all your kits around that topic or you can just have all kinds of kits for everything imaginable. Once you make up your mind, you need to have some kits available and ready to go before designing your web site. You need to stress the benefits of each kit. Make your customers feel that they have a need for that kit and they have to order it. Do not exaggerate. Your kit should be good enough to add a value. Testimonials are good marketing tools.

Some of these kits are just information. Others kits have parts with them. Kits with parts should be more expensive. You should run your web site as an e-Commerce site which means that you need to include a shopping cart and a payment system. You should keep adding more kits on a regular basis. Make one web page just for what is new in the kits world. Always search for new ideas that you can package as kits and put for sale. The more kits you have, the more money you will be making.

Your main source of revenue will be the selling of these kits. You can also accept advertising on your web site. Google AdSense can be a good source of income for you.

One word of caution is the fact that there are thousands of kits and projects online. You can't just take them, copy them and start selling them. That is totally illegal. What you can do is just take the idea, modify it and design your own. This is the way to do it if you want to stay out of trouble.

Chapter 48

Domains Web Site

There are lots of web sites dealing with the subject of domains. Some are selling domains. Others are registering domains and so on. You still can get a piece of the action and a piece of the cake too. A web site for domains can get very complicated. That is why I want to make it very simple for you. Immediately after the Internet just started some people spotted an opportunity to make a lot of money. What they did was to register a lot of good domains and turn around and sell them for huge profits and it worked very well. Some people registered thousands of domains and they get stuck with some of them. They can't sell them for the price they want and they can't afford to lose them. Your job is to help these people sell their domains by offering some tips that can help them market their domains and get some money for their investment.

Your web site will be very simple. It should have some information about such topics as what a domain is, how you can register a domain, how you can buy a domain, what makes a good domain, how you can appraise your domain, tips about selling your domain, how you can transfer a domain once it is sold and many other topics that have something to do with the subject of domains. You will have no technical difficulties setting up a web site like this. The biggest challenge for you will be the right content and the right information. You need to go very deep into the subject. There are lots of web sites that are offering just primitive information about the subject. You do not want to be one of them. Should you have the right information, you can build up a huge community because there are lots of people dealing with domains.

The only way to make money with such a web site is by accepting advertising. If you are dealing with domains, you can use the site to sell your own domains. All you need to do is to list them for sale. If you get a buyer, just negotiate a price. If you don't even have registered domains you can start buying them cheap and selling them for a profit. It could be a lucrative business for you. The market for domains is usually unpredictable. You can make a lot of money just by selling one domain. That is the only thing you can do in the domain area. If you want to do more you will need a lot of resources and that is beyond the ability of most ordinary people.

Chapter 49

New Products Web Site

There are hundreds of new products that that flood the market every day. Some of these products are worth buying; others are not. It is your job to look for the good new products, present them to your audience in your web site, recommend them and provide the link to the companies that are selling these new products. For each product you need to include at least one photo, detailed description of the product, what the product can do and why you recommend it to your audience. It is very important to be very honest in your presentation. Stay away from worthless inventions. A good invention adds value and makes our lives easier. There are lots of magazines, catalogs and directories that feature new products. You can also research the web for what is new. Go to Google web site and search for new products and see what you get. You will be amazed. It will take hard work to collect all the information you are looking for and to prepare it for posting to your web site. If you do not have the time to search and edit the information you need, it may be time to look for some help.

It is very important for your web site to look very professional. The photos you import to your web site should be very impressive and show a lot of details. Your new products list should be posted in categories so that your web site can be easy to navigate. Some of the categories that you should include are : New books, Electronics, New gadgets, Multimedia products, New tools etc.

Time is money and people are not ready to waste their time looking at something they are not interested in or do not have a real value. If somebody likes a product he can click the link that takes him to the company that is offering that product for sale. You can also cut a deal with some of these companies to sell their products for a profit. This can be a source of revenue for you. Also you can affiliate with all these companies that you are providing a link to their web sites, thus creating a second source of income. Every product you recommend to your audience can be a source of income to you. A third source of income is to accept advertising in your web site. You can easily apply to Google AdSense.

There are other possibilities that you can think about to increase your income. You need to be always on the look.

Chapter 50

Business Ideas Web Site

It is the dream of nearly every American to have his or her own business. One of the problems they are facing is the lack of real business ideas that can work. A lot of people have business ideas but they do not know how to put it to work. Basically they do not know all the details about how to implement it. The know how is very important. I give you an example. I was always fascinated with the digital sign business and I am still and I would love to know how it is done. I can not find a resource that tells me how to do it step by step with all the minor details. There are lots of things you need to know before you get yourself into a business. Hopeful thinking is just not enough. You need to know first how it works. You need to be familiar with the tools and parts you need and where you get them from. You need to know how to put these parts together and get your final product. You need to know how to program the unit and so on. What I mean is the technical details. If you buy one of these books about e.g. how to make ice cream, you will find almost more than 90% of the book has practically useless information about how to start a business, legal forms of a business etc. What is mentioned about the technical details of the specific business is practically nothing. I hate to buy a book that is supposed to teach you how to do something then I find the book discussing some crab like how to start a business, the business plan, forms of business, taxes and licenses etc. You need to know that everyone who is willing to start a business knows all these basics.

The way I do this web site is to come up with at least 50 hot business ideas. I list them in my web site. If you click on one of these business ideas you go to the web page of that particular business idea. This page will include a summary about that business. You will describe the nature of the business, the minimum money you need to start up with, the future of this kind of business and the degree of competition, how hard it is to start and so on. You do not need to mislead people because they are going to invest a lot of money and effort in that thing and they need a return on their investment. If your customer likes one of your business ideas, you will give him the choice to order either the e-book or the hard copy. The e-book should be less expensive than the hard copy because it costs you less and there is no shipping involved. An e-book can be easily downloaded and the customer doesn't have to wait for the Post Office man to show up by the door. I encourage my customers to buy the e-book by making it much cheaper than the regular book and remind him of the fact that he can get the information he needs immediately. You need to be serious about the information in the e-book. I am going to stress again that the customer doesn't want to know from you the basics of starting a business. Don't even mention it. The customer wants to know the fine details of how to start and run that particular business. If you do not give your customer all the details, you will not succeed. Testimonials are very important in that kind of business. Try to encourage every satisfied customer to post his comments and take their ideas into consideration by making the necessary changes. Even offer them discounts on their second order. A dollar or two will not hurt your business because you will be selling more. Customers' opinion is very important.

The best way to make money of this web site is to sell these e-books. A second source of revenue should be Google AdSense ads. I do not recommend that you affiliate yourself with any other web sites because, in this case, you do not know what they are selling. There are lots of scams on the Internet and you want to stay away this.

Chapter 51

Going Green Web Site

Going green is the wave of the future. We need to save the planet for future generations. We need to preserve our limited resources. We need to find new renewable sources of energy. This is the green movement. It is big and it is going to grow even bigger in the future. When it comes to this topic, I consider it to be very broad. If you want to get into this topic, you will need a lot of resources and a lot of help. There is too much information out there. Your web site should be filled up with articles about the subject. You need to encourage the green activists to discuss the subject in your blog. This blog should be part of your web site. Your blog should be updated regularly. Don't just depend on the members of your blog to contribute the full content. You post a subject that can create a debate or discussion among the group, thus enriching your blog.

Make a list of the good green products that you can offer for sale on your web site. There are thousands of them. This can be a good source of revenue for you. Your audience usually does not care about the price. They have a mission. Their mission is to save the earth.

If your web site is rich in content, easy to navigate, you will have a very loyal audience. This is a very strong movement and you should take advantage of this by being an advocate of this subject.

Advertising can be a second source of revenue for you. The ads that are accepted to you should have something to do with the environment and the green energy. I think a big part of your revenue will be coming from advertising.

The competition in this field is tough especially from the nonprofit groups. Who are actively soliciting contributions and have an army of volunteers. To compete with them you need to work hard and you need to hire some editors so the content of your web site will be better than your competitors. Having a blog linked to your web site will increase the audience of your web site and will help you with the search engines which will give a high ranking, thus increase your traffic more. You need to be patient because it will take a lot of time and effort to build your community.

Chapter 52

Go Solar Web Site

Solar energy is considered a big topic these days. It is one of the alternative energy solutions. As our President said, " Our dependency on foreign oil must come to an end.". To reduce our dependency on foreign oil, one big alternative is to produce more solar energy. One of the biggest problems facing solar energy now is the cost. It is more expensive to produce than traditional sources of energy but it is a clean source of energy. It doesn't pollute the environment as it comes directly from the sun. There are lots of energy coming to the earth's surface from the sun. That energy is enough to satisfy all of our energy needs. The problem is that so far we do not know how to harness it in a usable form in a cost effective way. This will be the challenge over the coming years. So far we have managed to make solar cells of silicon. These solar cells can convert sunlight into electricity. This electricity can be wired directly to the power grid to supply houses and business with their electricity needs. The idea of generating electricity from the sun is just not new. For decades, solar cells have powered calculators, satellites and even homes. The problem is that it costs too much to generate electricity this way than to generate it the traditional way. It is one hundred percent clean energy but still people care more about cost.

Solar energy is a very hot topic these days and in the future, not just for governments but also for individuals and groups. There is a very large and huge audience here and you can capitalize on this by having your own web site. Your job is to collect all the information on the topic and present it in your web site in a readable and attractive manner. For every article or piece of information ask your audience to post their comments. This will present your web site as a dynamic and continually updated one. This will help your ranking when it comes to search engines. Talk about the thousands of the products that are currently in the market and work by solar energy. Talk about how important it is to have clean energy like solar. Talk about the recent developments and attempts to cut down the cost of producing solar energy. Talk about government incentives for those who are willing to shift to the solar energy use. You will have huge audience and you can make enough money just from advertising. If you need more money you can sell books talking about solar energy. You can sell solar energy kits and plans. You can sell solar products and so on. You do not need a lot of money to build a web site like this but you need to spend a lot of time chasing all that new information. Probably, you will need help in the beginning unless you are on a tight budget and planning to do all the work yourself.

There are lots of web sites that are dealing with this issue but there is room for even more. Most of these web sites are nonprofits. There is a chance that they may not be competing with you. You can partner with. Even you can ask them to contribute articles to your web site. Your web site should contain information about solar energy in the form of articles, press releases and other forms of information. You will be selling solar products on your web site. There are hundreds even thousands of products that run by solar energy. You can't sell these products claiming that your products are cheaper in prices because they are not. May be the initial investment of your customer will be high at the beginning but in the long run they will be saving money. The selling pitch for products like these will be the fact that by buying solar products you are contributing to a more clean environment, you are producing less pollution and you are saving the planet for future generations. Most of the people who will buy from you have this concept in their minds. This is how you can build your marketing plan.

It will be a great idea if you include a blog into your web site. That blog should discuss the different issues of solar energy. Try to select the topics that stimulate a lot of debate and discussion. These kinds of information can encourage your audience to participate in your blog and enrich the environment. Update your blog on a regular basis with such articles as " What is new in solar energy ", " Government and solar energy " or " How we can reduce the cost of solar energy " and so on.

A big source of revenue for you will be from selling solar products. It can be a very lucrative source of income if you carefully select the products. Another big source of income will be advertising.

Chapter 53

Wind Energy Web Site

Wind energy is considered an important source of what is called alternative energy or renewable energy sources. Producing energy from the wind has a long history. It currently accounts for only one percent of the US electrical production. Despite of this, it is considered the fastest growing source of energy, representing a third of all new power generation in the US in 2007.

In 1985, Wind turbines in CA State produced enough electricity to power about 400,000 homes. Wind energy has gotten a boost when adopted by the Texas oilman, T. Boon Pickens. Pickens announced that he is going to build a wind farm in Texas that is likely to be the largest in the World. It is expected to be completed by late 2014. It will be able to produce 4,000 megawatt, enough to power 1.3 million homes.

The cost of producing energy from wind is continually decreasing. As the production costs are decreasing, wind and solar are beginning to approach the costs of other, more conventional electricity sources like coal. In 2005, it is estimated that it costs only 5 cents to produce a Kilowatt – hour of electricity from wind. The Midwest and plain states have the highest wind potential. Texas has a lot of potential and it is already leading the way. Wind energy is already attracting a lot of attention. New York City Mayor Michael Bloomberg is currently thinking of an offshore wind farm that could supply ten percent of the city's electricity needs within a decade. Also Congress extended tax credits for solar, wind and other renewable energies for companies and individuals.

With all the publicity of that subject it is your opportunity to cash in. With a web site that deals only with the topic of wind energy, you can build a very loyal audience. But you need to remember that your audience needs good information that is updated regularly. You need to include a lot of debates and all current news about the subject. You need to dig hard and research a lot to come up with the latest and greatest ideas. Your web site should be a place where people are able to share information and ideas about wind energy.

There are few places that sell and install these huge wind turbines. You can act as a dealer to them selling their products and services to your audience. You can make money from ads. You can make money selling information about that topic in the form of regular books or even e-books. You can make money selling the products and services of these companies. In all, you will have multiple sources of income.

Chapter 54

The Antique E-Shop

If you have a hoppy collecting antiques, you can change your hoppy to a business and make money of this. The idea is to set up an antique e-shop where people can list their antiques for sale and you charge them a fee for that listing. You can charge your customer a fixed fee just for listing the item for a certain period of time. You charge that fee whether the item is sold or not. For those who want to list a lot of items, you can charge them just an annual membership fee. If someone pays an annual membership fee he will have the benefits of listing unlimited number of items for free. You can take advantage of the site and list your own items. Go to garage sales, antique shops and other sites like eBay then buy cheap and sell high in your web site. There are still lots of people who really don't know the real value of the things they have and they offer to sell them just for any price; just to get rid of them. Even they give them away for charity.

To design a web site like this, you need first to have categories of antiques so customers can easily navigate your web site and find what they are looking for. Go to eBay and look at the antique category and see how eBay is dividing it into many subcategories. You can do the same thing. Although the idea looks very simple, you need a lot of technical skills to develop such a web site. You will also need to include a lot of tutorials and articles about antiques in your web site. You need to show your customers how they can make money dealing with antiques, how they can buy them cheap and sell them for a profit, how they can spot a bargain, how they can evaluate and appraise an antique item etc. The biggest problem for dealing with antiques is to know the value of the item that you are willing to buy or sell. You need to include a software in your site that enables your sellers to upload pictures of the items they are going to list. This is very important. You can't sell antiques without photos. One photo of the item may be not enough.

You can sell books about antiques. People will buy these books to learn more about antiques. You will be making money by collecting fees from your customers. You can also make money by selling your own antique items including books. You can make money from advertising. The good thing about this kind of a web site is that you do not have to deal with the final transaction between buyers and sellers on your web site. But you still have to include a shopping cart and a payment processing system to collect fees from your customers and to sell your own items. You can integrate PayPal and Google Checkout into your web site.

In order to succeed with this web site, you need first of all to be an antique collector and love what you are doing. You can't just come from nowhere and decide to deal with antiques. It will take a lot of long years to be good in that field. The second thing you need to have is the knowledge. You need to be an expert on the subject. You can sell your expertise in the form of lectures, seminars and other activities.

Chapter 55

Testing New Products Web Site

In this business, companies that have a new product will send the product for you to test and write a review in your web site. It is practically the same idea that Consumer Reports Magazine is doing. When you write a review about a product, you provide a link for your customers so they can click on it, go over there and buy the product. The benefit for the company is that it will get more publicity, more referrals and more sales. The benefits for you are numerous. The first thing is that you get to all the products you test. It is like getting a lot of things for free. The second thing is that you can make a lot of money if you affiliate with all these companies. You can make money every time one of your customers clicks that link.

For your web site to be successful, you need to look professional and act professional. You need to have the good tools to present the product for your customers in a best possible form. The companies donating products for you to test will be looking over your shoulder. They will visit your web site to see how their products are presented. The more professional you present yourself and your web site, the more expensive things you will be getting to test. Another point is that you need be very honest in your testing. Every product has its own positives and negatives. You have to mention both. You have also to develop a grading system that you can implement on the products you are testing. Have a copy of the Consumer Reports magazine or USA Today newspaper and check how they write reports on the products they test. You need to develop a system that is unique to your web site. Also you have to classify the products you are testing into categories so that your customers can easily navigate your site and find what they are looking for.

You can make a lot of money from advertising in your web site. You are in a situation to accept all kinds of advertising because your web site is dealing with all kinds of products.

In the beginning, you have to contact all these companies and explain to them what you are trying to do. This step is very important. It can make or break your business. Explain to these companies that you are working with a team of experts who are doing the testing. Mention to them the benefits they will get including the free publicity.

You will be also making money from the affiliation programs you will set up with all these companies.

Chapter 56

A Web Site for Consulting

There is an army of consultants over there especially in this country. If you are good at something you can declare yourself as a consultant in that field. You don't need a license to be a consultant. You don't need to be certified. All you need is to be a marketing genius to market yourself and get customers. It is a tough field because there is a lot of competition. But it doesn't hurt to try. My advice to you is that when you design a web site for consulting, do not depend just on consulting to bring you money. You may not be able to make decent money. You may not be able to make money at all. Try to diversify your income. Include other sources of income into your web site like advertising, affiliations, selling products etc. There are two ways to go when it comes to this consulting thing. If you are very good at something, you can just go ahead and start consulting in that thing only. The good thing about this is that you will have a niche. You will get only those customers who really need your service and are ready to pay top dollar for it. You will also get a high ranking among search engines concerning certain keywords. If you have good searching skills you can go for general consulting. What I mean by general consulting is that people can consult you about every aspect of their lives. You can also serve businesses too. If you ask me which way to go my answer is that I do not know. It all depends on you. The way to conduct that business is to charge your customers by the report. Say I am a customer and I am looking for a good college in the USA. I will have to fill up a form spelling what I need in as much details as I can. I submit the form with my payment. After few days, I get a report from you, about 2 to 3 pages, by email. You can send your report by regular mail but in this case, you need to charge your customer more. Should I need more information I should contact you and in this case the fees are negotiable depending on how valuable the information is, how hard to get it and so on. In this case you need to have a contract with your customer. Remember, you are selling information, so your fees are nonrefundable. If things go right, you can make decent money this way. You should include in your web site a lot of articles with very attractive titles in all sorts of information. Your articles should be very important to your customers' concerns. Your articles should be on the right side of your home page.

On the left side you should include links to your recommendations in every field of life like health, technology, electronics, photography etc.

If you want to include an e-store you should provide a link to it on this side e.g. " visit our store ". This way you will have multiple sources of revenue. You will have revenue from your consulting business. You will have revenue from your e-store. You will have revenue from affiliation with all these companies that you are recommending. You will have revenue from advertising.

Chapter 57

Corporate Gossip Web Site

Any web site that is dedicated to any kind of gossip e.g. celebrity, corporate etc will attract huge audience. In this setting, corporate include not only big companies like yahoo, Google and Microsoft but it can include celebrities too and anything that can generate news and debate. That web site is best done as a blog. Content is very important. You need to post things that can attract a lot of audience to your blog and generate a lot of discussion and debate. The success of your blog will depend on your content. Most of these gossips are rumors spreading everywhere. You get your material from someplace else like newspapers, magazines and other web sites. Don't try to make it up so you do not have legal responsibility. You need to provide a very attractive title to each posting. You can offer RSS feed in your blog. By law, you will have no legal liability for what is posted in your blog. It is under the freedom of speech act.

The big question is how to turn that blog into a money machine. You will have huge audience who have the time to read the gossips and post their own gossip. Probably they can have the time for other activities in your web site. You can make money with advertising. There is no question about that but you need to explore other ways to generate revenue. The ads usually appear on the right side of your web site. On the left side, you can include your recommendations for your customers. You can categorize your recommendations and add a link to each company that is offering a product or a service. I give you an example. If I click on a link in your web site about e.g. Web Hosting, I go to the page that displays the best companies that you recommend for web hosting. If I click on one of them, that will take me to that company web site. You will have affiliations with all of these companies. This provides you with another source of revenue. Another idea is to have a store that can sell things that you think your customers will be interested in. This can be another source of revenue. In this case your site should be e-Commerce capable which means you need to have a shopping cart and a payment processing system.

Chapter 58

Helping Hand Web Site

A lot of people want to do different kinds of things but they don't know how. I want to start a web hosting company but I do not know the technical details. I want to set up a shop to make stained glass but I have never done this before and I do not know how to do it. I want to start a business to build and install solar panels but I do not know even what solar panels look like. In all these case and much more, there are hundreds, may be thousands of people who have been through this everyday of their lives. They know the stuff, they have done it and they have a proven record. They can help you get started and do whatever you want to do for a fee, of course. Your job is to bring these two groups together. This is how to design your web site. You have two groups of people; those who are looking for a solution and those who have the solution. Those who are looking for a solution are allowed to list, post and advertise what they need for free. Anyone who wants something can just come to your web site, list in details what he wants, how big his project is, his budget, how much he is willing to pay for the help he will be getting and so on. Those who can offer the solutions should register in your web site. The registration is not for free. They have to pay you an annual fee or membership fee to have access to your data. Also, they can post their profile on your web site, including their skills and what they are capable of doing. Also, they are allowed to make offers on the different projects that are posted on your web site. You can make it simple this way. It is better not to interfere in the deals between both groups. More interference means more headache. It is the responsibility of both parties to close the deal together. Your job is only to bring both parties together.

Your biggest source of revenue will be from collecting these membership fees. Of course, you can have additional income from advertising. Also, you can have a long list of companies that you recommend to your customers. You can join their affiliate programs and make more money that way.

Chapter 59

Distressed Businesses Web Site

Any business that is operating at a loss is considered a distressed business. There are millions of businesses that deserve to be called distressed businesses. A distressed business has one of three options to make it. The first option is to try to modify itself in a way that helps to make money or at least to break even. This is usually what a distressed business tries to do first. If this step doesn't work the owner will try the second option which is to try to find a buyer. There are lots of people who are looking to buy distressed businesses. They think they are bargains. There are lots of benefits if you do your homework. The best benefit is that they will pay much less than the company really worth. Since most of these people think that the problem with these distressed businesses is usually the management, they believe that they can turn them to profits by having a new management. The third option is to let the company goes bankrupt. In this scenario there is an opportunity for you to make money. All you have to do is to design a web site that brings the buyer and seller together. The owner of the distressed company will advertise the sale of his business or whatever he wants to do in your web site. You will charge him a fee. He has to post as much details about his business as he can to attract buyers. Every distressed business should have its own full web page that shows all the information about the business and a contact number. You can classify these ads into categories. For example, one category is for tech companies. When I click on this category, it will take me to all the distressed companies for sale in this category. When I click on one of these companies, I go to another page that spells all the information about that particular sale. The prospective buyers or visitors are allowed into your web site for free. Your job is to get the buyer and seller together to make a deal. Once they get together, they are on their own to close the deal. You can charge the distressed business owner a one time fee of $100.00 for the lifetime of the ad. This will be the main source of revenue for your web site. You need to include some articles in your web site e.g. how to buy a distressed business, how to sell a distressed business, how to fix a distressed business and so on. Another source of revenue for you will be from advertising. You can sign up for Google Adsense and this way you get more revenue.

Remember to keep your web site looking as professional as you can. This is the golden key to attract traffic and make money.

Chapter 60

Special Group Interests Web Site

There are thousands of special groups or groups with special interests in the real world. I give you a lot of examples. People who like fishing are a special group. People who have diabetes are a special group. People who are overweight are a special group. Antiabortion activists are a special group. I can name you thousands and thousands of these groups. Your job is to target one of these groups in your web site. The first thing to do is to select a target group. That is a very hard task. Selecting the right target group can make the difference between success and failure. Make a list of the groups you like. It will be much better to deal with something you like or you feel you belong to. Make another list of the groups that you think they make a good target group. A good target group is made up of people who are online most of the time, are loyal to their group and have money to spend. You don't target a group whose members don't even know how to use a computer. You don't target a group whose members don't have the resources to buy anything. This way you will not be able to make any money. Look at the two lists you just made. If a name of a group is listed in both lists, put that name in a third list. Discard the first and second list and look at all the groups in the third list. They are all good targets. Choose the best one. Once you choose your best group, study and research the group very well. Everything counts. Check their habits, hobbies, age, gender, marital status, what they like, income etc. Based on all the information that you collect, design your web site accordingly. Your web site should have the information and activities that are important to them. Your web site is better designed as a blog or it should have a blog. This will encourage group participation. In this blog, you discuss things that are important to the group and let them post their comments.

You can recommend products and services to the members of your group and provide a link to each of these products and services. At the same time you can affiliate with these companies to provide you with a source of revenue.

You can include an e-store in your web site where you can sell selected items that you think the members of your group will be interested in buying.

You can also sign for Google AdSense to get some revenue from advertising.

Chapter 61

The Rich And Famous Web Site

We all love to be rich and famous. We love the way rich people are living. We love their style and their way of life. If you don't believe me, look at how popular " The Rich & Famous " show is on TV. We want to know how these people live. We want to know how they spend their money. We want to know what their houses look like. We want to know what they like and what they hate. We want to know what they like to eat, what they don't like to eat, what their kids look like, what their spouses look like, how they make their money etc. There are lots of things about rich people that a huge audience would love to read about.

You can build a web site on that subject. Your web site would be just traditional or classic. It is better done using the blog format. The main content of your web site should be in the middle of the main home page. You need to have a lot of great photos. In fact your content should have more multimedia than text. People want to see rare photos of their beloved stars. If you have the resources you can include some video clips. If you have the blog format, your audience will enrich the site by posting their comments. You should update the contents of your site on a regular basis, at least once a week or you will not be able to build up a large community. As I mentioned before that content occupies the middle of your site. The left part of your web site should contain links to services and products that you recommend to your audience. These links can help you earn some revenue by joining the affiliation programs offered by these product and service providers. On this side too, you can include a link to your e-store where you can sell selected items that can appeal to these groups of people. The right side of your web site is usually left for advertising using Google AdSense. This way you will have multiple sources of revenue.

There is a lot to learn from reading about the lives of these rich people. How they rise from the bottom to the top is a very interesting thing. Most of these rich people were not born rich but they have made their way to the top. There are lots of lessons to be learned here. Some of them are considered role models to a lot of young people. You have to be very careful about your content. It has to be interesting and educational at the same time.

Chapter 62

The Rise of a Great Company Web Site

Very few companies in this world have a universal impact on the whole globe. Look at companies like Microsoft, Google, Yahoo and others. These companies have changed the world. Their impact will be felt for ever. These companies are very popular all over the world. You can capitalize on this popularity and change to a money machine for you. Make a list of the effective and very popular companies and pick up one of them. It will be better if you pick up one you like. For me personally, I like Microsoft. I believe this company has changed the world to the best.

It is very easy to design a web site for this project and you still can make a lot of money of it. The content should include history of the company and its founders, current CEO, the impact of this company on the whole world and what this company is currently offering to the public in terms of products and services. You should have great and very attractive titles.

The way to make money with this kind of a web site is to have your own e-store selling the products and services of this company. You can also include books written about the company, T-Shirts, mugs and other things that is related to the company. If you choose a company like HP or Dell, you need to contact them to explore the full range of services and products that they offer. Try to sign up for a dealership to get a discounted price or direct drop shipping to your customers so you do not have to keep inventory.

You will have to accept advertising in your web site to generate more revenue. Google AdSense is easy to sign for and easy to implement.

It is very important to select a company that is very popular among the general public. The company should have the ability to generate a lot of talk, a lot of debate, a lot of gossip, a lot of unexpected news and so on. It also has to have a lot of competitors who are trying to knock it down. It means a company that is always generating a lot of news. Best companies that fall in this category are: Microsoft, Yahoo, Google, Dell computers, HP and others. Every one of these companies is great to excellent in what it offers to the public and its impact is everywhere. These are just examples. You can pick up whatever you feel it is going to work for you.

Chapter 63

Specific Technology Web Site

People of all ages are crazy about technology. We live in the age of the Internet and since then people believe that the human being is now capable of practically doing everything and anything. We invaded the space then we invented the Internet and now the whole world looks like a small village. There are lots of technologies everywhere and there are groups or followers of every one of these technologies. There are people who are interested in the satellite technology, others are interested in robots, still others are interested in cloning and so on. These different groups are everywhere on the Internet. If you are interested in a specific technology , you can start a web site discussing that technology. For example, if you are interested in the robots technology, you can create a web site that is just specific for that technology. You have to include all the details about the subject. The way you discuss the subject should encourage young people to come and join. These young people should be the future generation for that technology. For the web site to be unique, you should discuss that subject only, nothing else. So when it comes to robots your site should be number one on the list for search engines. This site is better done with a blog platform in mind. This way audience and members can post their own comments and ideas. You should encourage them to even contribute with articles. You need to include multimedia in your site in the form of audio, video and photos. Designing your site as a blog will actually help you. You do not have to do all the work by yourself. Your audience will contribute to the success of your web site. You need to update regularly with fresh ideas that appeal to your audience. For those who are new to the field and they like to get into it, you should include tutorials about the basics of that specific technology that you are adopting in your web site. There are lots of contests and prizes that are offered by different organizations and associations in any particular technology, you should look for this and mention it in your web site. One best source of revenue for you is to sell your skills. With all that knowledge that you will be having in that field, you can consult, give lectures, seminars and even write books.

Another source of revenue is advertising on your web site. You can even go more by selling some products to your audience that is closely related to the specific technology that you are promoting. You can sell some kits that people can use to build small projects.

Chapter 64

Specific Industry Web Site

You can build a community around a specific industry. To succeed you have to be in the field and you know the ins and outs of that industry. I warn you about selecting a broad subject. The bad thing about choosing a broad subject is that search engines will hardly recognize you. I give you an example. If you choose farming as your favorite industry, the subject is fine. Farming is the oldest industry in the history of the human beings, but the problem is that the subject is too broad. You have to narrow your subject as much as you can. It is better to discuss growing vegetables than farming in general. It is best to select growing tomato or herbs. This is what I mean by narrowing your subject.

Every industry in the world has its own audience whether that industry is big or small. When selecting an industry you have to figure who your audience will be. Do they have Internet access or not. This is the big question. If they are not active users of the Internet, no one will be reviewing your site. There are lots of industries that people can rally around. Some of these are very old, some are not. For me I choose an industry that can add a real value and it doesn't require a lot of capital to get into. Your first step is to go to the Google search engine. Search for " Industry Associations ". You will get a list of the most important industries. Make a list of what appeal to you. Then choose the one that you think you can build a community with. Tools industry or auto industry is a good choice but I am afraid that it is too broad.

Designing your web site will be just straightforward. You have the content in the middle of your home page. You need to include a lot of information that can attract a lot of audience. Many people would like to get into a specific industry, your web site should help them by offering the right information. The right side of your web site will be for advertising. You need to accept advertising so you can build up some revenue. On the left side you can offer your recommendations for products and services. You provide a link to each of these companies. Later, you can affiliate with these companies to generate another source of revenue. Also you can use your skills in the field to provide consulting, give speeches, lectures and seminars. If you have a chance to sell products and services that are related to that particular industry, you can just go ahead and start your e-store. You can sell kits, books and other products.

There are very important topics that you should include in your web site that people care about. People would like to know if they can make money with that specific industry. They want to know the future of that specific industry. They want to know what it takes to get into that industry. If you can start small, how much capital you really need. This way your web site will be very informative.

Chapter 65

A Web Site for a Specific Country

Though the economy now is in a downturn, still Americans love to travel. Even with the swine flu in Mexico, Americans have never stopped travelling to Mexico. Travel is a way of life to most Americans and nothing will stop that. You can take advantage of that fact by picking up one of the countries that Americans love to travel to or a country that you expect Americans will start visiting after they read what you got in your web site. Most Americans love to go to Canada, Mexico and Europe. The rest of the world is mostly unknown to the Americans. Some other countries like Egypt, India, and Turkey are fascinating with their old history and deserve to be visited a lot. And there are other good places in the world too. You can pick up one country that you think it is unique and build your web site around it.

Your web site should contain all the details that are important to the visitors of that country. You should mention why we should visit, current attractions, how you can travel to that country, people's customs and habits, Best time of the year to visit, how friendly the people over there are and important phone numbers. Your web site should have detailed direction to visitors stated in a step by step way. You site should be the number one online reference to that country.

You can make a lot of money arranging group trips. You can do this by partnership with the local tourist agencies in these countries. This can be a good source of revenue for your company. The locals in these countries would love to partner with you. Even the government will pay you to promote their countries in a positive way. Remember that tourism can be a big source of revenue for these countries. You can even import all kinds of products from this specific country and sell them on your web site. This can be another source of income. Of course, you can advertise in your web site. You can sign for Google AdSense and this can be a third source of revenue to your organization.

A word of caution is that I advise you not to interfere with politics. Stay in your field of promoting friendship and exchange of visitors. A lot of these foreign countries consider politics as interfering with their internal affairs. They can accuse you of all kinds things like spying etc. You don't want to go this way. You want just to make a living.

Chapter 66

A Web Site for a Specific Star

We all have our own role models, stars and celebrities. They do not have to be just movie stars. Lots of them are inventors, politicians, tech titans and so on. Thank god, we all are different. That is why every one of these stars has his or her own audience. Make a list of the well known people that you like. Select one of them. The one you choose has to have a lot of audience in order to succeed. You can choose, for example, Bill Gates, George Washington, Elvis, Jane Fonda etc. All these people are real stars and have a lot of audience.

Your web site should contain a lot of information about that star. You can add a blog to your web site. This will generate more debate and discussion. In your blog post the controversial issues about that star that will lead to even more debate. Include lots of photos. Also, you can include audio and video clips.

You can include at least three things to get revenue from a web site like this. The first thing is to post your recommendations for products and services to your audience. For example, where they can get the best service when it comes to web hosting or other services. You can also recommend different products. You can recommend as many services and products as you can. Remember that your audience is just human beings like you and me. They need services and they buy products. For every company you mention in your web site, provide a link to it, so your customers can click that link. Every time one of your customers clicks a link you earn some money. It might be a small amount of money but it will add up and you end up with a good source of revenue. Think about all the things that have something to do with your star. You can sell all these things in your e-store. Some products you can buy at a discount and sell them for profits. Others you can make them yourself and sell them for even a bigger profit. Be creative and make a big long list. Look at other web sites and see what they are doing. Nobody is building a web site just for the fun of it. Everybody wants to make money of his web site. You can get lots of ideas just by visiting these web sites. Don't forget to have a pen and a piece of paper and write down everything you see that makes sense to you.

A successful e-store can be a good source of revenue for you. Another source of revenue is to accept advertising. Your web site should sound professional and look professional. There are lots of free photos all over the web. You can download a lot of them. Use only those that are related to your subject.

Chapter 67

Membership Web Site

A membership site is a web site where your audience pays fees to get into your site. The fees are usually paid on a monthly or annual basis. People sign up and they choose an ID and a password. Every time they come to your web site, they have to log in. There are very few web sites that charge membership fees. The one I visited was Safari.Com. This web site has thousands of technology books that you can read online instead of buying these books. In return, you pay a monthly fee. Since technology book are very expensive to buy, it is a win win situation. Safari.Com web site is already has thousands of members. You have to come with a great idea like this to succeed with a membership site. You have to offer something that is very valuable. You have to offer something that people really need very bad. You have to offer something that people want not just once or twice but on a regular basis. If you look at the example of Safari web site, their idea is a success because they offer something that is very valuable and people need it on a regular basis. If you can't offer something with these three specifications that I previously mentioned you are wasting your time. Another place that is charging membership fee is GoDaddy.Com. You pay an annual fee. The best thing to do is to go to Google Search Engine and search for membership sites. Go visit each one of them and check their ideas, may be you can copy some of their success. If you find an idea that you think people will pay membership for it, go ahead and do it but keep in mind that the membership fees will be your main source of revenue. The more members you have, the more revenue you will get.

Can you sell something to your members?. I do not know the answer to this question. It all depends on your idea and your subject. In some situations you can, in others you can't. People will buy from you if they are very happy with your site, they trust you and you are offering something they need.

Even advertising will not be a great idea. People will be afraid to click on any link because it will take them away from your site and, to come back, they have to login again.

As I mentioned before go to other membership sites and see what they are doing. Then you will have a good idea about what works best for you.

Chapter 68

Kids Web Site

Having a kids' web site is a lot of fun. Before you start designing a web site for kids you need to ask yourself this question: Why do kids go online?. Most of the kids go online to have fun. Most of them go online to play games. Some of them go to sign for contests and free stuff. Older kids go online to communicate with their friends and do other activities. That is why social networking is exploding. Very few kids go to web sites mainly for educational things unless advised by their parents. The good thing is that the purchasing power of the kids is growing. When they insist on something the parents usually give up and buy them what they want. You can use this to your advantage.

The first thing you need to do is to design a web site that is very attractive to kids. This will require a lot of resources and talents. You need to hire high tech people who have good web development skills and excellent design expertise especially with regard to designing web sites that are totally dedicated to kids. You need to invest in expensive software. A kids' web site is not going to be cheap. The first thing to include in your web site is all kinds of games. There are lots of free games to download all over the Internet. Pick up the best and post them in your web site. There are games designed for kids only and there are games for both kids and adults. Including this last category of games will help bring the kids and their parents together. Most of the games in your web site should be offered for free. Few excellent games should be offered for a fee.

The second thing to offer in your web site is sweepstakes, contests and free stuff. There are thousands of companies that are offering sweepstakes, contests and free stuff. List them in your web site and offer a link to each one of them so your audience can go and sign.

Up to this moment, the only revenue that you are getting is just coming from the paid games and that will not be enough. You need to create other sources of income. One good source of revenue is to open an E-Store in your web site where you can sell things that are in high demand by kids. You still need to study what kids really need and like. This is how you make a sale in your web site : when kids see something they like in your web site, they just ask their parents to buy it for them and they insist. Make a long list of the hot items among kids and offer them in your E-Store. If you get it right, this can be a good source of revenue for you.

You can also recommend services and products that have something to do with kids and you can affiliate with the companies that are offering these products and services. This can be a good source of revenue for you. Another great source of revenue for you is advertising. Google AdSense can be very successful in a web site like this.

Chapter 69

Before You Go Web Site

Though the whole world now is like a small village, thanks to the Internet, we are still different. People in every country have their own habits and customs that are different from yours. What is considered polite here in America can be rude somewhere else. Even in the same country, there are differences between the east, west, north and south. In global economy there is lots of travel. If you are travelling somewhere to another country for any reason, it will be nice to know the habits of the people over there. You don't want to be taken by surprise or look like an idiot because you do not know what these people like and what they hate. That is the idea of this web site. So far I have never seen that idea on the Internet. To do this web site, you need to search every country in the whole world and list what every country's people like, dislike and post your recommendations for anyone travelling to that country. It will be a lot of work in the beginning but once it is done, you don't have to update anything. If I want to visit, for example, a country like Egypt, all I do is to click on Egypt. This will take me to the web page dedicated to Egypt. In the web page I expect to find all the travel information related to that country including habits, customs, what is considered right and what is considered wrong over there, and so on. Your web site will have huge audience because you are offering a free service that people need on a regular basis. You can have multiple sources of revenue. Every source of revenue can be huge. Take advertising, for example, you can have advertising on every single page. Your web site will be huge because you are going to cover more than 100 countries and communities. With every single web page you can post your recommendations concerning services and products that are important to those who travel. Provide a link to each company mentioned in your web site, affiliate with them and you will have another great source of revenue. Should you need more revenue, you can have your own e-store selling products that appeal to travelers. However I do not recommend this last step for two reasons. The first reason is the fact that your web site is already huge and you don't want to make it bigger and you will have to hire more people because it will be too much work for one person. The second reason is that, in order to have an e-store you will need the e-commerce software which is considered an added expense. But if you have the energy and the resources to do it, there is nothing wrong with adding another source of revenue.

For every country you need to post, in a separate web page that is linked to the main web page, what I call a country profile. In this profile, you mention a summary about that country. That summary should include the following: a recent map for that country, population, income, habits, major cities, condition of the infrastructure, relation with the USA, degree of hostility, climate, best time to visit, places of interest etc. You also need to mention the laws and the travel rules. Then you mention the customs and habits and, in the end, you need to mention your recommendations. A lot of photos is very essential to your success including maps and photos of places of interest. You can get a lot of help from the government in these countries because it is in their interest to attract more visitors to their countries.

Chapter 70

Seniors Web Site

If you create a web site for seniors that covers every topic concerning seniors, probably you will not have any chance for success. The subject is too broad and there are thousands of web sites for seniors fighting for a high ranking among different search engines. You have to narrow your subject as much as you can. To help you pick up a subject that concerns seniors, I am going to talk about seniors and what they care about. Health and money are the two important issues that seniors care about most. Seniors are always having health problems and they are looking for magic cures. Seniors are afraid to die and they want to live longer. Some seniors, especially women, do everything possible trying to look younger. A lot of seniors are depressed and they want something that makes them happy. A lot of seniors feel lonely and they want to be entertained. As for money, most seniors are generally retired and they have no earning capacity. They are looking for ways to save money and spend less.

Even if you create a web site talking about money issues for seniors or health issues for seniors, it is still too broad of a subject. When it comes to money, there are thousands of web sites dealing with this issue, so you are better off dropping it of your list. Make a long list of the health issues that concern seniors. There are hundreds of them. You will be surprised if I tell you that there are millions of seniors who are continually searching the web looking for solutions to health problems. These millions of people will be your audience. Pick up a subject like how to improve your memory, how to look younger and stay younger, how to live longer and so on. Build up your web site on one of the subject like those I just mentioned. You will have a lot of visitors and you will enjoy a high ranking among different search engines. After picking up a subject, post everything you find about that subject in your web site. The information you post should be in a very categorized and simple manner. It will be better to post your information in big size letters or font so seniors can look it up easily. The content of your web site should be displayed in a very attractive manner. The main content of your web site should occupy the middle of your page. On the left side, you can post your recommendations for products and services that seniors need. Seniors are always on the look for services like life insurance, auto insurance, discounted medicine etc. Any company you recommend for a service or product, you provide a link to it, so your visitor can click the link and go directly to their web site. You can make some money affiliating with these companies.

On the right side of your web site, appears the Google Adsense ads which can provide you with another source of revenue.

Chapter 71

Stressed out Web Site

There are millions of people who are stressed out because they can't cope with the difficulties of life. There are lots of factors that can lead to stress. Lack of enough money is one of them but it is not everything. You can be very rich and you still can suffer from stress. Money can't buy happiness. The symptoms of stress can vary from one person to another. Some people suffer from anorexia i.e. they do not want to eat. Others, on the other hand, eat too much to a degree that they become over weight. Some people feel unhappy all the time. Others feel tired all the time. The most serious effect of stress is when some stressed people try to kill themselves or try to inflict harm on others.

If you create a web site dealing with stress, I assure you that you will have huge audience. In your web site you need to teach people how to handle stress. You need to show them how to handle stressful situations. Concentrate on how to remedy stress without taking any medicine. There are lots of behavioral therapy models that can be applied to stress. You have to explore every avenue that handles the problem but stay away from medicines and drugs. Hundreds of books have been written about the subject of stress. You can go through these books and post what you think is going to work. The best way for a web site like this is to be in a blog format. This will be a great way for dealing with the problem because when you post something new about stress, you get feedback from your audience. This can enrich your web site. With all the huge audience you will be having, you can have multiple sources of revenue. Since you will be an expert in handling stress you can arrange for seminars that can bring you a lot of money. There are lots of qualified people who are just giving seminars about how to handle stress. They even write best seller books. You can do the same.

Another source of revenue is advertising. You can accept advertising in your web site. Advertising can be a good source of revenue since you will have a lot of traffic to your web site. You can also recommend products and services to your customers. Put a link in your web site to each of these companies, then affiliate with them. Every time a customer clicks on one of these links you make money. Another source of revenue is to have your e-store. Look for products that can appeal to this group of people. Your credibility is on the line here, so only selects products that work and have benefits to your customers. There are lots of products in the market with false or unproven claims. Stay away from these kinds of products. They can do more harm than good to your reputation. You need to make money but you should be honest in the first place.

Another thing I want to mention is the role of religion in combating stress. Religion can play a big role in this situation. We all know the fact that most of the people who attend religious meetings on a regular basis are generally more happy than those who are not. They are more satisfied with their lives and they are less stressed. You need to research the relation between religion and stress and post your findings in your web site.

Chapter 72

Free Things Web Site

This is a very easy site to create. All you have to do is to search the Internet and look for web sites that are offering free stuff, sweepstakes, contests and surveys. Hundreds of companies are offering free stuff, contests and sweepstakes as a form of advertising and marketing. Also, surveys can be part of a marketing campaign. Usually people will never waste their time to take a survey unless they get something back in return. So you can have three categories in your web site to attract traffic. Each one of these categories can have subcategories. Your audience will be mostly kids, teens and poor people who have lots of time on their hands and they can do a lot of clicking which is good for advertising and affiliations.

Make sure to update your web site on a regular basis. If a contest is over, delete it of your web site. You will be busy all the time updating your web site. You need to advise your customers not to use their regular email address or their home phone number because this is what telemarketers are going after. Create a Yahoo email and use it.

There are two ways to make money with a web site like this. You can make a lot of revenue through advertising. As I told you before, the kind of visitors who will come to your web site are those who have lots of time and the good thing, they can do a lot of clicking which you can translate into income by posting Google AdSense ads. These people are also looking for bargains, so make your recommendations for all kinds of products and services that are considered bargains. These people will be more than happy to click and explore the different offers. For every offer you recommend provide a link that your visitors can click on to take them to that offer. You can affiliate with all these companies and this way you can change these clicks into cash. It could be another source of revenue for your web site.

I visited lots of web sites doing same thing. You need to visit them and check out what they are doing before you design your own web site. Try to figure out the ways they make money with a web site like this. You can copy their success. There is nothing wrong with this. With the current economy the way it is, you will be surprised about how many people sign to take a survey, sign for a contest or sign for something that is free.

Chapter 73

Education Web Site

I do not mean by having an education web site to start an academy or online university. This will take a lot of resources which most of us don't have. What I mean is very simple. There are lots of centers, web sites and associations that are offering seminars and courses. Most of these courses are online courses. Some of these courses are offered for free, others are offered for a fee. For example, HP is offering good free courses. At the same time, HP is also offering courses for people who want to work on HP products like maintain and repair HP copy machines and other products. These courses are not free. Dell computers is also offering all kinds of courses. These classes are mostly offered online. There are other companies and associations which offer all kinds of seminars. I always receive a catalog from a company called Learning Tree International. Their web site is : HTTP://www.LearningTree.com. This company is offering what they call hands – on training for managers and IT Professionals. They are offering over 225 in-depth courses in the form of seminars for 2 to 3 days in different cities in the USA.

You can list all these online courses and seminars in your web site and provide a link to each. You can even negotiate with each of these providers to send them applicants for a fee. You can provide an application form for people to apply for the courses they want, then they click a button which takes them to the provider's web site where they can pay the fee. Part of that fee will be for you. You can negotiate a separate deal with each of these providers. Some of them will just pay you for referral. Others will let you register applicants, collect the fee and take a percentage. In either way, you will be making money. If you are going to be a full partner i.e. you going to register applicants and collect fees, there are lots of work to do. You have to post a full description in your web site for each of these courses or seminars. This way people will know what they are going to do and what to expect. Your web site will be like a big directory for this kind of activity on the web.

Always think of other ways to increase your revenue by including other activities in your web site like advertising. You can sign up for Google AdSense. It is very easy to sign up for and very east to set up. If you are going to register applicants and collect fees you have to have a shopping cart and a payment processing system. In this case you can think of adding an e-store to your web site. You can sell educational materials like text books, CDs, DVDs and other things that appeal to your customers.

Chapter 74

Colleges Web Site

Do you know that there is a fierce competition among American Colleges to attract foreign students. A big part of the income of any American university is just coming from foreign students enrolled to take different studies on a degree or non degree basis. You can take advantage of that competition and make a lot of money of it. Colleges and universities will pay you to bring foreign students to their campus. You can create a web site to help foreign students come to study in America. For a nominal fee, a foreign student can post his profile in your web site, you study his profile then you match him up with at least ten universities. Besides your recommendations, you ask these colleges to send him information. Also, you need to send him your recommendations and he should do to increase his chance of being accepted in one of these colleges. These recommendations are considered very valuable because every college has set certain criteria for students to be accepted. They do not just accept anyone who can afford to go to college. He has to meet specific standards. After this you help the student apply for these colleges. After being accepted you get paid by the college. You have to make agreements with the different colleges first. You tell them that you are in the business of bringing foreign students to study in the American colleges and universities and you need a piece of the cake. You can concentrate your efforts in just one country. It is better to be your native country. For example, if you, your parents or grandparents came from china, you can work with Chinese students. This will be much easier for you and you can even offer more services to these students. You can help them get the student visa. You can arrange to relocate them and help them from the moment they arrive in the airport till they get familiar with the life in America. You can offer to solve their problems and answer their questions. You charge these students some fees for your services. Also, you will be compensated from different colleges and universities.

Probably you can make some money from advertising but I do not think it will be too much. You need to include a lot of articles about college education in America. You also need to include what life looks like for college students in USA. Include lots of photos from different campuses all over America. You want to attract as many students as you can. Also, include testimonials from previous students who got help from you.

Explain to the students the legal steps involved in coming to America as a student. Explain to them how to apply for a student visa and what papers they need.

I don't think there are lots of web sites doing this activity. So I expect to have very little competition.

Chapter 75

Information Web Site

Most people go online looking for information. We are living in the information age. The amount of the information on the web is huge and that is the problem. It will take you hours and hours to find what you are looking for. People are looking for information on thousands and thousands of topics. If you are going to build an information web site, you need to pick up only one subject or topic. No more than one. Your subject needs to be unique, have a lot of audience and there are lots of services and products that are associated with it. For example, if you pick up a subject like fishing, it is considered a unique subject. There are millions of people who love to go fishing and there are lots of services and products that can be sold to those people who love to fish. The problem with fishing is that it may be too broad of a subject and therefore you can expect a lot of competition. Same thing applies to topics like TVs, Digital cameras, hunting etc. In selecting the right topic, you need to follow the criteria I just mentioned. After picking up the subject that you think it is the right one, start by collecting as much information as you can about that subject. Present that information in your web site in a simple easy to go through manner. Your articles should have very attractive titles. Include lots of photos. You need to position your web site as reference number one when it comes to that topic. The idea is that when someone searches the web for that subject, your site will come on the top. This is how you win.

All that information should occupy the middle part of your web site. If you are not good at editing, you need to hire someone to edit that information for you so you can present it in a very attractive and pleasant way. The right side of your web site should be left for advertising. You can sign for Google AdSense to get some revenue from advertising.

During your search for information about your subject, try to think about the products and services that have something to do with your subject or topic and can be sold to your customers. You can have your e-store to sell as many as you can of such services and products for a profit. Anything that you con not offer for sale in your web site can be recommended by you. Make your recommendations to your customers concerning all these services and products and provide a link to each of these companies. Contact these companies and join their affiliation programs. This way you can generate another source of revenue.

Chapter 76

Recycling Web Site

So far I have not seen a good web site on that very important subject of recycling. What I mean by a good site for recycling is a web site that helps people start their own recycling business. The two important issues that can translate into serious business opportunities are recycling papers and recycling plastics. I do not think you need a lot of investment to recycle papers or plastics. At least, you can get the papers and the plastics for free. The problem is that most people they do not know how. There are very few resources talking about this. Even these resources are old enough and very complicated to grasp. There are lots of new machinery that can do the job more efficient in a cost effective way. When you create a web site for recycling, your job is to explain to people step by step how to start a business that actually recycle plastics or papers, not just the collection part of the business. You need to mention the tools and the machines that they will need. Also, talk about the start up money and the different government incentives. There are lots of programs on both the Federal and State levels that encourage recycling. These programs range from grants to low interest loans. There are also tax benefits.

If you want to make money of this web site, you need to write books and sell them on your web site. The first book should be about how to recycle plastics. The second book should be about how to recycle papers. You can write a third book about financing a recycling business. Offering these books for sale on your web site can generate a lot of income for years to come.

You can also include in your web site other business tips in general. This will differentiate your web site from other recycling web sites. Try to build your site with business in your mind. Some of the business topics that you should include in your web site are: how to write a business plan, how to finance your business, legal aspects of a business and so on. You do not need to include a lot of details on each of these topics. Your main mission is how to get people to start a recycling business and make money with it. This will be the main goal of this web site. After publishing your web site and your books you will be an expert on the subject. This will open the door for you to make even more money consulting, giving seminars and speeches and selling your new skills. It will be great if you actually start a recycling business of your own.

You can also recommend products and services to your customers. Remember that your customers will be starting a business, so they need products and services that can help them in this field. For each company you mention in your web site, you can provide a link for it so that your customers can click that link to check out what these companies have to offer. This click can generate income to you through affiliation programs. You can also accept advertising on your web site. Google AdSense can be a good source of revenue for you. This way you will have multiple sources of revenue if you build a great web site that attracts a lot of traffic.

Chapter 77

A Web Site for Women

When you create a web site dealing with women issues, you should not target all women. This will be a very broad subject. You can't even target a specific age group of women. It is still too broad. You need to narrow your topic as much as you can. You can target for example, overweight women, black business women, Latino business women and so on. It will be even better if you target a group that is smaller than these groups. The group of your choice should have the qualifications that can help you make money with your web site. Members of this group should be in the habit of going online a lot. They should have a high purchasing power. You do not want to create a web site for a group of people who do not even go online. This will be a waste of time and money.

After selecting the right group, try to find out the issues that are important to them. These issues will be the main content of your web site. Discuss these issues in your web site. If among these issues are concerns or problems, post solutions to these concerns. If there are needs try to satisfy these needs. Do your best to keep your target group coming back and forth to your web site. One good thing that can keep them engaged is a good content. Another good thing is to offer them the things they need at a discount price. Find out a selected number of products or services that your target group will be interested in and offer them for sale at your e-store. This can be a good source of revenue for you. You can't offer everything in your e-store. So your next step is to recommend other products and services to your customers and provide a link with each product or service. Your customers can click on that link and it will take them to the service or product provider. If you affiliate with these companies, these clicks can generate income to you.

An easy way to get some more revenue is to sign up for Google AdSense advertising. It is very easy to set up.

The design of this web site should be straight forward. If you do not include an e-store, it will not cost you a lot. You will be just paying for the web site hosting. But if you include an e-store, other costs will be added. The key to success is to pick up the right target group and to have excellent content that can attract this group to your web site. If your target group is narrow enough, you can get a high ranking among different search engines. If you get a high ranking, you will get a lot of traffic. Good content and high traffic will translate into greater revenue.

Chapter 78

Presentations Web Site

This web site can be a great source of revenue for you. It works like this. Suppose you are a great programmer. You can sell your skills in this web site. All you need to do is to translate your programming skills into action, with a computer that is loaded with the right software and microphone to record your voice. You can record episodes of programming presentations and courses. The software program will record what is going on in the computer and your voice at the same time. You can explain what you are doing using the mouse, the keyboard and of course your voice. After you finish recording you can review and edit then post your episode on your web site for download. You can make your episodes just 20 minutes each. The software you need to do something like this can be downloaded online. Some of the software are offered for free and some can cost you money. One free software, called camtasia at www.camtasia.com, is good enough to do the job. It is an open source software but can work with windows.

You can execute this idea not just with programming but with any kind of skills you have and you think it is worth money. If you know Microsoft very well, you can do unlimited numbers of episodes and post them in your web site for customers to download. If you worked, for example, in a factory that manufactures solar panels and you know the process from A to Z , you can put it in episodes and post these episodes on your web site. Your first episode will be about what a solar panel is. Your second episode will be about how these solar panels work. Your third episodes will be about the parts you need to manufacture them. Your fourth episode will be about the tools and machines you need to put them on. Your fifth episode will be about how it is done. Your sixth episode is about how to connect them together and so on.

You need to have a clear voice and good language skills. You need to know how to communicate well to your listeners what you are trying to do. A lot of people are very good in what they are doing but they do not know how to explain it to other people. They are not good speakers. In this case you need to hire somebody else to do the explaining part.

Depending on how valuable the information you are presenting you can charge your customers a membership fee to download your episodes. The good thing is that a web site like this can open the door for you and give unlimited chances for greater revenue. People who need that kind of skills will know you and try to contact you with all kinds of offers. You will be making money all the time. At the same time, you can sign up for Google AdSense advertising to grab another piece of the advertising revenue. You can post your recommendations for products and services, provide a link for each of these companies and affiliate with them to make even more money. There is nothing wrong with building your own e-store in your web site. Since you already have a payment processing system installed, all you need to get your store up and running is the shopping cart. You can sell products and services that are close to your main activity. For example, if you are making episodes about Microsoft Office, you can contract with Microsoft to sell their products and services. This can be another source of revenue for you.

Chapter 79

Writing Skills Web Site

When it comes to web sites, content is king. If your web site has a lot of good content, it will naturally attain a high ranking among different search engines. The problem is that despite the fact that lots of people have great ideas that can bring lots of money, they do not have the ability to translate these great ideas into a good readable content on their web sites. They don't have the required writing or editing skills. You will be surprised if I tell you that this is a widespread problem. If you have good writing skills, this can be a goldmine of opportunity for you. You can tap into this unlimited market by designing a very good attractive web site and tell your customer this: " If you want a web site as great as this one, just contact me, I can help ". The content of your web site is your passport to this unlimited source of revenue.

In your web site, you should talk about the value of a good content to a web site, the way you present information can make a big difference. You talk about the services you will be offering to your customers and how these services can help them money and make their lives much better. You will be working by the project, so don't post any fees or prices on your web site. Your customers should contact you with what they really need, then you will agree on a price. Assure your customers that your service is fast and everything is done electronically. Your editing and writing skills are not just for web sites' content. You can edit book. You can edit speeches. You can edit reports and you can even write ads. If you are talented in this field, your potential earning power is practically unlimited. You can even write an e-book about how to improve your writing skills and sell it on your web site. This can be another source of revenue for you. A third source of revenue is to sign up for Google AdSense ads. You can get some revenue out of that.

If you have writing skills you will be smart enough to think of other ways to generate more revenue out of your web site. You have great tools under your belt, you should use them. You can even receive big projects from big corporations trying to update their primitive web sites. There will be lots of work waiting for you that you may think of hiring more people to give you a hand. All you have to do is be focused on your mission and try to be the best.

Chapter 80

Making Money with Business Networking Sites

Probably you mar heard about the social networking sites on the web. Although you still can make money with these sites, as I will explain in another chapter, their main goal is to build social communities. Another group of web sites that is growing fast is what is called business networking sites. These web sites are mainly specialized in building business communities. The most well known so far is www.LinkedIn.com. Others are:

http://www.illumio.com

http://www.doostang.com

http://www.plaxo.com

And others.

For the purpose of this chapter I will focus my discussion on LinkedIn. LinkedIn is a web site that has been designed with the objective of connecting business minded people in an efficient way that lets them share information, get more deals and prospects, increase their customer base, promote themselves and their businesses, get answers to their questions and inquiries and other business issues.

To take advantage of what is offered in LinkedIn, the first thing you need to do is to sign up to create a new LinkedIn account. All you have to do is to fill up the application form the click the " Join LinkedIn " button. This will take you to the " Contact Settings " page where you will be asked about the way you going to use LinkedIn. After this you will have a free LinkedIn basic account and a LinkedIn member home page. The free account is your chance to test the water and see if LinkedIn is the right thing for you. You have three choices. You can cancel any time you want. You can stay the way you are with your free basic account. Finally, you can upgrade your account to what is called " Premium Account" for which you have to pay a monthly fee.

After you sign in, the first thing you need to work on is to create your profile. Once you complete your profile you have the choice to make it visible to only certain LinkedIn members or to make it public to anyone on the web. Since this is a very essential part of your presence on LinkedIn, You to spend some time to learn how to write a great perfect profile. The best thing is that you can always update your profile anytime you want. Remember that your presence on LinkedIn is a continuous learning experience, so this is a good chance for you to update your profile accordingly. A very important thing is to make your profile public so everyone on the web can see it. LinkedIn automatically provides a URL for each member's profile page. That URL looks like this http://www.LinkedIn.com/in/1234. It is better to change your URL profile page to:

http://www.LinkedIn.com/in/yourbusiness.

The second activity that you can do on LinkedIn is searching. You can search for real people, real businesses and real companies. You can search for a product or a specific service. You can search for specific jobs and so on. LinkedIn with its huge membership can be a valuable searching tool. There are lots of available searching techniques on the site. You need to experiment with all of them.

The next step is to start building a contact list. You can invite any member or non member of LinkedIn to join your contact list. As you keep adding new connections your list grows bigger and bigger. LinkedIn gives you a way to remove a connection that you no longer need. LinkedIn can be a valuable resource for finding jobs as well as for finding qualified people to fill up open positions. To take full advantage of the tools that LinkedIn offers in that field, you need to create a very effective profile.

Another great thing about LinkedIn is that it is a place where you can ask questions and get answers from other LinkedIn members. LinkedIn can be a fantastic tool for those looking for information to start a business, to design a project or even something concerning your personal life. You can also view other people's questions. LinkedIn even encourages every member to participate in answering other members' questions. LinkedIn even provides you with a number of ways or methods to contact other members even if they are not in your contact list.

There are thousands of LinkedIn groups that are mostly created around a common hobby, interest, background or business. You can join any of these groups that you feel it is of interest to you. You can even create your own group and invite other members to join.

As you can see business networking sites offer you unlimited chances for success and profits whether you have a web site or not. If you have a web site or a business, you can use these tools to promote your business and your web site. This is in turn can bring you a lot of sales and translate into more revenue. If you do not have a web site you still can take advantage of the unlimited opportunities offered by such sites as LinkedIn. These opportunities can be in the form of jobs, leads, contracts, deals etc. So you still can make money if you take the right move.

Chapter 81

Making Money with Video Sharing Web Sites

When talking about video sharing web sites, the first thing that will come to your mind is www.YouTube.com. Of course, this is the biggest and most well known but there are some other smaller video sharing web sites. Some of them are:

Http://www.Guba.com

http://video.yahoo.com.

http://uncutvideo.aol.com

http://www.blip.tv.

http://www.veoh.com

http://www.howcast.com.

And others.

Since all of these and the others that I did not mention are nothing compared to YouTube, this chapter will discuss only YouTube.com. But you should check the other video sharing web sites on your own.

In most cases, to make money with YouTube, you need to have your own independent web site. If you don't have a web site and you do not have the intention to make one you still can make money by using YouTube.com and I will show you how later in the chapter. You need to understand that you can't buy or sell directly on YouTube.com. The idea is to attract traffic from YouTube.com to your site. You need to change video viewers on YouTube to buyers on your web site. The first thing you need to do is to go to YouTube to see how that web site works and what different businesses are doing over there. Study all the details and write down all the good ideas. Try to copy the success of these businesses. The next step, even before you think about producing your videos, is to be part of the YouTube.com community. When you subscribe to YouTube.com you will have what is called MY Account page. That account link appears at the top of any YouTube page. When you need to go to My Account page you just click on that link. Part of your account is what is called YouTube's channels. When you post your first video, you create your own YouTube channel. Other users can access your channel to see all the videos that you have uploaded. Also, users can subscribe to your channel to receive notification when you upload new videos to the YouTube.com site. Your channel can be the best marketing tool for your web site because YouTube viewers can access your channel page to learn more about you and to connect with your business. The most important information that you can include in your channel is your email and a link to your independent web site. If someone goes to your channel and likes what he sees he can click the subscribe button to subscribe to your channel and this way can be automatically notified via email of any new activity on your channel.

You can't just post some videos and expect to automatically get a lot of viewers. You have to be very active in the YouTube community. You need not only to view and subscribe to lots of other channels but to leave comments on the videos that you view. Also, you can invite them to view yours and may be they ask their friends to do the same and so on.

Another form of community on the YouTube.com is the YouTube group feature. Each group is interested in certain types of a topic and exchange ideas, share videos and have discussions. Find out the group that best represents your business or interest and join them. You can even create your own YouTube group and invite other people to join your new group.

If you have a presence on the social networking sites like www.FaceBook.Com and www.MySpace.Com , YouTube makes it easy to send videos to these sites. This is another way to drive more traffic to your videos. You can also upload your videos to other video sharing sites on the web.

To generate revenues from your YouTube videos, the first thing you need to do is to create high quality videos that have value for people to watch. How to videos are very popular. Also, entertaining videos are popular too. A video that has commercials in it will never attract any attention. So my advice to you is to work hard to produce a video that can attract potential buyers of your product or service. The second thing is to include the URL of your web site or even a toll free phone number upfront in the title card for the video. You can even include the price of the product or service, any special offers and how to order in the title card. This way people will have the chance to go to your web site where you can close the sale.

If you don't have a web site and you do not have the intention to build one, you still have a chance to make some money using video sharing web sites like YouTube.com. There is more than one strategy. The first strategy is to present yourself as a professional to businesses to help them marketing their businesses using video sharing web sites. The second strategy is used in case you are selling something for example on eBay. If you are selling products on eBay, you can link directly to your YouTube videos. Also, if you are bidding on projects on elance.com, you still can link this to your YouTube videos. This way you get more customers.

There are lots of details to be covered beyond the scope of this book. So if you are interested in that field, you need to dig more into it.

Chapter 82

Making Money with Social Networking Sites

Social networking sites help people communicate in a variety of ways. They can add new friends. They can join groups. They can share information ranging from photos to invitations to events and even classified ads. And there are many other activities that can be shared on these sites. The way to make money with social networking sites is to promote your business and your web site, turn traffic to your web site and increase your sales. If you do not have a web site, you still can use the social networking sites to make money. I will show you how later in the chapter. Currently there are many social networking sites on the web with FaceBook.com and MySpace.com being the top two. When it comes to social networking sites, they currently have hundreds of millions of users. This way they are considered a powerful marketing channel. Social networking sites are giving marketers new abilities and valuable tools to target the right audience. Social networking sites are helping advertisers to stop wasting ads on people who will never buy. This way they help them making their ads cost effective by going directly to the target groups. The number of wasted ads will be minimal thus a lot of money will be saved.

Social networking sites can also be a great recruiting tool. There are hundreds of millions of well educated and most qualified job candidates who are currently members of these sites. If you are looking to fill up some vacant jobs, this is the place to be looking for the candidates. At the same time, if you are looking for a job, you can find one through these sites. To use social networking sites for business, you need to build a strategy for yourself. First of all, you are not allowed to buy or sell anything on these sites. Your primary goal is to drive people from over there to your site where they can do activities like buying, selling, signing for something and whatever you want them to do. You need to have a continual presence on as many social networking sites as you can. Set up realistic goals and objectives. The way to succeed is to present your product or service as a distinguished brand, then your second step is to build a community around your brand. Your community will give a valuable chance to improve your product if you pay great attention to their feedback. The community you are building will also help you market your product through testimonials, referrals and word-of-mouth marketing.

As I mentioned before, there are hundreds of social networking sites out there. My advice is to concentrate first on the big two : www.FaceBook.Com and www.MySpace.Com. I will talk about FaceBook.com and you can take it as an example for all of the social networking sites.

To establish your presence on FaceBook.Com, the first thing you need to do is to set up a FaceBook page. To set up a FaceBook page, you need to sign up for a FaceBook account. After signing up for an account, you can create a new page. It is an easy and straight forward task. FaceBook provides you with a template. All you have to do is to add your content. You can also add photos, videos etc. You can add a link to your web site and provide your email address. If you are selling something on eBay, for example, you can add a link to it. Try to make your FaceBook page as entertaining as you can. Make your page public so everyone can see it. You can add all kinds of gadgets to it like games, contests etc in an effort to increase the chance of engagement and interactions. The purpose of your FaceBook page is to recruit customers. Make sure that everyone knows about it. A very popular technique is to include a link to your page in your email signatures and web site if you have one. Update the content of your page and respond to your fans. People will keep coming back to your page if they are expecting something new. You can have as many different pages for different situations as you can. Suppose you are marketing two different products. You can make one FaceBook page for each product. Each page is appealing to a different kind of audience. You can create targeted ads on FaceBook and the rate is much cheaper than the Google AdWords but there is no guarantee that these kinds of ads will increase your sales.

If you do not have a web site you still have a chance to use social networking sites to make money. One way is that if you are looking for a job, social networking sites are a great recruiting tool. It is a great place for job applicants. All you have to do is to create a great profile for yourself and post your resume. If you are an active seller on eBay, you can link your items directly to social networking sites. This will increase the chance that your items will sell. If you are an application developer, you can make money by building applications and widgets that are designed to be used by FaceBook members. You can even teach people how to build applications for FaceBook.com and other social networking sites. Social networking sites have developed a platform that allows users and developers to create new functionality and widgets. According to FaceBook.com, more than 20,000 applications were developed on its platform just in the first few years of its life. The majority of FaceBook.com members have installed at least one plat form application in their profile. Companies and businesses of all kinds are developing all kinds of applications for social networking sites. Some of these applications are offered as free downloads, others for a fee.

There is a lot to learn about using social networking sites for business purposes. It is beyond the scope of this book.

Finally I would like to mention that there are more social networking sites than FaceBook.com and MySpace.Com. Hi5.com appeals to non US countries especially Latin America, Europe and Asia. Friendster.com is the most popular social networking site in Asia.

Chapter 83

Making Money with Google

Google Is considered the biggest search engine in the whole world. There are lots of things that are offered by this giant. Actually, if you want to discuss Google you will need a whole book for this. Since we are concerned with how to make money with Google, This will be the only topic to discuss about Google in this book. There are lots of ways to make money or save money with Google. I will have to discuss them briefly. If you need more information, you can go to the Google web site where there is a wealth of information.

Google Apps: Provides a set of tools that you can use to manage your business through your web site. The standard package is free. The first tool is the Gmail. You can sign up for as many accounts as you need at http://gmail.com. The second tool is the Google calendar where you can organize your appointments and schedules. The third tool is Google Docs. which looks like Microsoft Office. The fourth tool is Google sites where you can build up a free web site for your business. Google even offers you the tools to build that web site at http://sites.google.com. The fifth tool is Google talk which is a communication tool that lets you do instant messaging, communicate with people just about anywhere they are and share documents and photos.

Google Search: Google is number one search engine on the web. About two thirds of all searches are done through Google. Understanding how your customers use Google is the key to the success of your business. A great thing to add to your web site is Google search. Google offers a tool called a custom search engine that lets you add a Google search box to your site for free. This is a great thing to add to any site whether large or small. This will give your site more credibility and more power. You can find about this by visiting Google's Custom Search Engine home page at http://www.google.com/cse.

Google AdSense: This is what concern a lot of people because this is where the money is. You can sign up for free as long as you have a web site. With this program you can earn money when you let Google display different ads that are relevant to the content of your web site. These are highly targeted ads and you make money when the visitors to your web site click on these ads. It is very easy to set up and it is one of the best ways to make money online. For more information and how to sign up you need to go to the Google web site.

Google AdWords: If you have a web site and looking for traffic Google AdWords is the best program for you. You pay only when people click on your ads. AdWords offers you instant access to more than 75% of Internet users in USA alone. The best thing is that there is no minimum spending limit and you set a maximum daily spending so you do not exceed your budget. Your ads will appear on thousands of web sites with potential visitors and you can get results very soon. Another good thing is that you can change your ads or even your account any time you like. There is no doubt in my mind that the best cost effective way to market your business is to use Google AdWords ads. These ads are pay per click, very effective and the advertiser pays only if the user clicks the ads. A typical payment is just few pennies. Web site owners are now building successful businesses using the traffic they get on their web sites using Google AdWords ads. You can get more information at: http://adwords.google.com.

Google Base: Another free product from Google is Google Base. With this tool, you do not need a web site to put your stuff online for sale. Simply describe your items on Google base to make it as easy as possible for people to find them when they search. You can sign up for Google Base for free. Popular item types that you can list are: products, events, activities, vehicles, housing and jobs. It is like free advertising. Google base is considered a free Google service that helps you virtually publish any kind of information. To post an item to Google base, you just go to Google base and choose a category then post your information. You can use this program to sell anything, look for anything and advertise just anything. You do not need to have a web site to use it and make money with it. You can go to Google base at: http://base.google.com. I would like to mention that you can add your products on item at a time or you can add multiple items at once.

Google Checkout: If you have an E-Commerce web site, you will be doing much better adding Google Checkout as a payment method. It is free and it can be big help in building trust. I talked about Google Checkout in a separate chapter.

Google Maps: At http://maps.google.com.

It is a great tool that helps you enhance your business and makes it easy for your customers to find your business. Part of the Google maps is the Google maps local business center where you can add your business information to the local business center which makes it easy for your customers to find your business. Submit at:

http://google.com/local/add. You can even upload photos and videos to your listing.

Even Google gives you the chance to attract more customers by giving you the ability to create online coupons and offering them to your customers as printable coupons. Your customers can get the coupons through your Google maps at http://maps.google.com/coupons. All you have to do to create your coupon is to sign in to your local business center account at: http://google.com/local/add. Then click the coupon tab and follow the directions. If you are using Google Checkout as your payment method, your coupon can be processed using Google Checkout.

Google Gadgets: These are pre-built small applications that are available for you to add to your web site. There are thousands of Google gadgets that are available for you. You can find the most popular in http://www.igoogle.com. Google even helps you to create your own gadgets and makes inserting Google gadgets in your web site a very easy process.

And there are many other services that Google offers. What concern you mostly as a beginner are the services and tools I just mentioned. If you do not have a web site and you are not planning to have one, you can use Google base to sell products, cut deals and even sell your skills and look for jobs. It is like free advertising. You have to close the sale by yourself.

If you have a web site, you can make a lot money using Google AdSense. You can use the low cost advertising, Google AdWords, to drive more traffic to your web site. You can use Google Checkout to get paid. There are all kinds of details on the Google web site. You need to go through all these details before making a decision. And if you have time you can read about other tool that Google has to help your business.

Chapter 84

Making Money with Yahoo

Probably Yahoo.com is the number one web site on the web when it comes to the number of visitors and the way its web site is amazingly designed. Yahoo.com is a web site that is rich with information, very easy and pleasant to navigate and contains a lot of individualized information. When compared to other top web sites like Google or Microsoft, Yahoo site is, without doubt, much better. Just have a look at " My Yahoo " page, where the registered users have a chance to select exactly the information they want to see. There are lots of free information and that is why everyone is going to Yahoo. I have no doubt in my mind that over 99% of Internet users have a free Yahoo e-mail.

If you want to know what yahoo can offer you and how you can make money with Yahoo, just go to Yahoo Business Section. Yahoo can offer you web hosting for a very reasonable price. Yahoo even has the tools to help you build a very professional web site in a very short time. You will have to learn how to use these tools but this doesn't take a lot of time. There is no secure and reliable service like yahoo.

If you want to sell online, you can quickly and easy create an E-Commerce web site. Best of all for Yahoo is the fact that they offer their customers 24 hours phone support. Also, Yahoo is offering unlimited site storage, unlimited e-mail storage and unlimited data transfer with every web site. Yahoo Merchant Solutions can be a great start for you especially if you are not tech savvy.

Like Google, Yahoo is trying to make money of advertising and helping you, at the same time, to market your web site and attract more visitors. It works like this: You create your ads for display in search results. Interested customers search for what you sell. They see your ad, click it and go to your web site. The big three to advertise with are Google, Yahoo and Microsoft. Which one is better, I can't tell you. A good idea is to try them all with a small amount of money, then you decide which way to go.

You need to go to http://www.yahoo.com and study all the details of the site and figure out how to use the site to help your business and make more money.

Yahoo site has been a pioneer for the Internet revolution and it is still a great site for people and businesses.

Chapter 85

Making Money with Microsoft

Microsoft is another big giant company with an amazing history. Without Microsoft we will not be the way we are now. There is no doubt that Microsoft has contributed a lot to technology.

The question of the chapter is how to make money with Microsoft. There are many ways to make money and also to save money with Microsoft.

First of all, Microsoft is offering free e-mail to practically everybody on earth who can apply for it. That is a good thing. Another great thing that you should take advantage of is the fact that in an effort to compete with its rival, Google, Microsoft introduces a program called Office Live Small Business. With this program you can get a free web site, a free e-mail and also a free web site hosting. When it comes to domain name, you are allowed to use your own domain if you have one, something that is not available with the free web site program offered by Google. If you do not have a domain, you have two choices. The first choice is to register your own domain for $14.99 a year. The second choice is to accept a fourth level domain that is free. It will be looking like this: http://yourdomain.web.officelive.com. With this program you can create a high impact business web site with free templates and easy to use tools. You do not need any technical skills. My advice to you is that it is a good deal and you should go for it. Use your own domain. Another point is that this free web site is not an E-Commerce web site, so you can't make money with it selling products or services. The only way to make money with a web site like this is through advertising and affiliations. Also, if you have a business and you want more exposure for your business, you can apply for this program and have a free web site for your business. This is the way to go. It will not cost you a dime.

Another way to make easy money with Microsoft is to try to sign a dealership with them to sell some of their products. You can make a fortune just selling Microsoft Office. If you go to eBay you will find a lot of sellers selling Microsoft Office. They call themselves certified Microsoft dealers. You can be one of them. Most of them are selling the academic version of Microsoft Office, which is offered by Microsoft at a cheaper rate only to students and instructors. You can do the same thing and make a decent income. You need to follow exactly the terms of your dealership agreement with Microsoft or you will not be for business for too long. If you are dealing with software especially the academic version, you need to sell this version only to students and instructors. If you do otherwise, Microsoft has no mercy.

There are many other opportunities with Microsoft. You need to go to their web site and explore all the details. You will find out real opportunities.

Chapter 86

A Graphic Designer Web Site

This is a perfect business for those who want to work from home. A graphic designer does all kinds of things. You can make logos, business cards, labels, reports, brochures, catalogs, restaurant menu etc. You can easily earn between $60,000.00 to $120,000.00 easily from your home using your mainly your web site. These days, graphic designers do work in multimedia, graphic design, visual communication, advertising, animation, web development and they use computers to create their designs. The goal of a graphic designer is to communicate an effective message to the audience using a combination of text, logos, graphics, newsletters, brochures, posters, photos, images, signs or any other way. Graphic designers develop the final layout and production design for magazines, newspapers, journals, corporate reports and other documents and publications. Most of their work now is to develop materials for the Internet e.g. web pages, interactive media and multimedia projects. The occupational outlook for graphic designers is great especially those with web design and animation experience. Graphic designers must be familiar with the latest computer graphics and design software. Most of the work now is not printed work but all forms of electronic media. It makes a lot of sense, at least in the beginning, to specialize in a graphic design area that you know very well then expand to other areas later. Once you determine the type of graphic design business you want and if there is a market that you can serve in that specific area, it is time to start setting up your shop and your web site.

You can do low cost marketing e.g. you can offer to teach a course on graphic design at your local community college or present a seminar at a local chamber of commerce meeting on how to design e.g. a newsletter. In both of these activities, you can market your name, your services, your business and your web site. This way you could actually produce some income.

You can offer editorial services in addition to graphic design services. You can present yourself as a one stop shop for e.g. newsletters (design, proofreading, editing, writing, e-mail newsletter creation, printing even delivery or shipping). You can add to your services desktop publishing (complete publishing of manuals, books, newsletters etc.). You can expand to animation and web site design.

With your web site there will be multiple sources of revenues. You will be making money of the services you are offering to your customers. The best way for you is to charge by the project. You can advertise in your web site and you can join affiliation programs. You need to pay a lot of attention to your competition and what they are doing because it is a very competitive field.

Chapter 87

Federal Programs Web Site

Do you know that there are thousands of federal programs that people don't know anything about. There are programs for helping small businesses, programs for housing, programs for energy and the list goes on. Your jib is to explain to people all about these programs. You should show them how to take advantage of these programs. Also, a good idea is to provide links to the government sites that offer these programs. You can also provide articles in your web site about the available federal programs. Very important is to show people how to apply for these programs.

You can sell reports to your audience. These reports should have a value and people should benefit from them otherwise, you will be gradually losing your audience. No one wants to pay money for a product that is practically has no value. The titles of your reports should be very attractive to buyers. Or you will have difficulty selling them. Some of the great titles are : Free government money, How can you buy government land for pennies on the dollar and so on. You can even sell e-books. This can be a good source of revenue for you. Another source of income will be advertising.

You can also work as a consultant for individuals and businesses who want to apply for government grants, low interest loans and contracts.

The content of your web site is very critical to your success. You can't just have a web site with just a list of links. This will not work. You should provide your audience with all the details about different federal programs. Also, provide a long list of good links that your audience can click to go and get more information. You can present all your information in the form of different categories so your web site will be easy to navigate.

Chapter 88

Making Money with Amazon

It is very easy to get started selling on Amazon. Practically every one can do it whether you are a business or just an individual. Suppose you are not a member of the Amazon Market Place and you have a book you want to sell. You can view the price of the book on Amazon. All you need to start selling your book is to click on the " Sell Yours Here " button. Then you can fill up the necessary information and provide your banking details so Amazon can transfer the money from your sale to your account. Now you are an Amazon Market Place seller. It is that easy. You can review all of your activities at your " Seller Account " page at: Http://www.amazon.com/seller-account.

Amazon offers 4 levels of seller programs. As a beginner, you will be concerned with the Individual Selling Account. Anyone with a regular Amazon account can click the " Sell Yours Here " button on any Amazon product page to offer a used, new or collectable item for sale. In contrast to eBay which charges basic fee for listing, there is no listing fees but Amazon collects a 15% commission on each sale.

Generally, there are two ways to list an item for sale. You can go to your " Seller Account " page then click on " Sell Single Items " . The other way is to search for the Amazon page for the product you are offering then click the link " Sell Yours Here ". It is very important to provide an exact description of your item. Also, follow the Amazon guidelines for rating your product (new, very good, good, refurbished, acceptable, unacceptable).

To set your price, you need to go as low as possible compared to other sellers, if you want your item to sell fast. A good thing is that Amazon collects the money from the buyer's credit card or checking account and deposits it to your Amazon Payment Account, where you can you can transfer the funds to your own bank account. You can do that transfer once every 24 hours. You are going to ship the item at your own expense and Amazon will give you a credit for shipping.

Each time you list an item, Amazon will send you an e-mail confirming your listing. Amazon does the same thing if one of your items is sold. Also, Amazon provides you with a set of tools to manage your inventory. Generally, your listing will expire in 60 days but you can relist them again.

A great way to start on Amazon is to list used items like books. You can make decent money by selling these items which you can get very cheap from garage sales, estate sales, auctions and even library sales. Make sure that your items are new or close to new. This will increase the chance of your items being sold.

There is a long list of forbidden items that you can't sell on Amazon. You need to review this list. You need to take good care of your customers because their feedback can affect your business and can have a direct impact on whether you fail or prevail.

There is a lot more details to selling on Amazon. What I just presented to you were the main points to get you starting, then you can learn more by practicing. You do not need a web site to sell on Amazon and you do not lose any money if your item doesn't sell and this is a great thing. Amazon is considered the biggest competitor to eBay. It has a lot of traffic and a lot of sellers prefer to list on Amazon due to the fact that it does not charge any listing fee. So it is better for you to start on Amazon then expand to eBay and other sites.

Chapter 89

Making Money with Content Driven

Web Sites

This type of web sites is best represented by : http://www.eHow.com. EHow.com is a great place that is specialized in short articles about how to do just about anything. There is also eHow's how to videos and there is also how to community. It is free to use eHow.com services. The site makes its money mainly by accepting advertising.

If you are interested in writing and you have the writing skills you can publish articles on eHow.com and make money in return. The first thing you need to do is to register with eHow.com and create a username. Once you are a member, you will be able to write articles, add comments on articles and interact with eHow.com members. The second thing you need to do is to sign up for the " Writer Compensation Program " and then start writing. Once you are enrolled in the Writer Compensation Program, all of your articles are automatically eligible for payment. There is no charge to sign up and whenever you submit your article for publishing, it goes live on the site immediately.

EHow.com will pay you through PayPal. As part of the Writer Compensation Program sign up you will be asked to set up a personal account with PayPal if you are not already a PayPal member. EHow.com will deposit your monthly earnings into your personal PayPal account before the end of the following month. If you earn less than $10.00 a month, eHow will carry over that amount and pay you once your earnings exceed $10.00. You can always go to " My Earnings " page to see how much you've earned. You get paid by article. Your article's earning potential can be based on a combination of several elements including the amount of times it's been reviewed and its category. The more useful your articles are to the readers, the more money you could make. Technically, there is no pay range per article. One good way to attract a larger audience and possibly make more money is by adding photos to your articles and be more active in the eHow community. To get you started, eHow.com offers a lot of tips and guidelines to how to write effective articles. Also, eHow.com has a page on eHow's most-requested topics. Every article's earning potential is essentially based on its popularity. So, the more useful your article is, the more popular it might be and the more money you could potentially make. If you want your articles to get the most exposure, the first thing to do is to go through the few tips offered by eHow.com.

It is very easy to publish how to articles on eHow.com. Just sign in to your eHow account and from your profile page click on the " Write New " button. From there eHow's publishing wizard will guide you through the publishing steps. You can edit and delete articles after being published. You can also add photos and images to an article. There are article submission guidelines on eHow.com that you must follow. Make sure to go through these guidelines before you start. Plagiarism is considered a serious problem that faces many online communities and eHow.com takes that problem seriously. Make sure to read about what is considered a plagiarism and totally avoid it. EHow.com gives you the chance to rate any eHow article and even add a comment. Also, you can report any offensive content in an article. EHow.com introduced what is called eHow points. By earning points, eHow members can increase their member rank from novice to enthusiast to authority and then master. You can earn points by writing more articles, when you add images to your articles and earn even more points when you write articles that were requested by other members. A high ranking brings you more viewers to your articles and this way you make more money.

EHow.com has forum groups where you can get news updates about the site and familiarize yourself with the eHow community. Also, eHow.com has different groups that you can join. You can even build your own group. Creating a personal profile is a very important part of your successful presence on eHow.com. Once you have joined the eHow.com, you can create a personalized profile to promote yourself or your business. To get started, go to your profile then go to the " Edit Profile " page. Click on the " Edit Profile" page. If you would like to add a little more personality to your profile, click on the " Edit Interests " button. Here you can provide additional information about you and your life and let everyone in the community knows about it. You can edit your personal profile anytime you want and you can also add personal images.

Also, eHow.com offers you the chance to add friends to your friend list. To add other eHow member to you friend list, visit his/her member profile and click the " Add as a Friend " button. The member will be sent a message notifying him/her that you would like to add him/her. Once he/she accepts your request, he/she will be added to your list of eHow.com friends. You can also remove a member from your friend list.

The amount of money you can make varies depending on the number of good articles you publish. EHow.com claims that the site has already paid millions of dollars. If you submit a lot of good articles on a regular basis you could end up making few thousands of dollars a year which is not a bad deal at all.

Chapter 90

Making Money with Elance.Com

Elance.com is a great web site for those who want to work by the project. If you have a special skill you can make money with your skill using Elance.com. First you need to present yourself as an expert in that area e.g. you are an expert in producing podcasts. Before you start marketing yourself, you need to find out as much as you can about the market conditions. There are certain skills that are in high demand. An easy way to find the underserved markets is to visit the Skills Central page in Elance.com to learn more about the skill demand in general.

Elance.com offers the following categories: Web & programming, Design & multimedia, Writing & translation, Admin Support, Sales & marketing, Finance & Mgt, Legal, Engineering & MFG. Each of these categories has about 40 to 50 subcategories of skills and job assignments that you can bid on. You need to get familiar with these categories. Browse them one by one and list all the skills that already have.

The first thing you need to do is to sign up. To submit proposals and be listed in the Provider Directory, you must first sign up for an Elance provider account, pass the Elance admissions test, verify your phone number and create a profile. To sign as a provider, follow the steps below:

Click the 'Sign In or Register' link, then click on the 'Sign Up Now' link then click on the 'Become a Provider' button.

Choose the type of plan. Type Individual or Business, depending on the size of your company and how much work you will be submitting proposals for on Elance.com.

Select your membership plan. There is no long-term contracts, no sign up fee and no termination fees. You can cancel and upgrade anytime.

Choose the category in which you would like to offer your services. You can add more than one category but in this case you will have to pay additional fees.

If you would like to build a team of providers on Elance.com you can check the box and agree to the additional charge for this added functionality. You can think about this and if you like this feature you can add it later because it will cost you money.

Review your selection and click continue. Create a username, a password and enter your company name. After this, you add your primary contact information including a phone number.

You can choose whether you wish to be listed in the Elance.com directory and whether you would like to receive communications from Elance.com. You must agree to the Elance terms of service in order for your account to be created. Click continue when finished.

If you selected a paid membership plan, choose your payment type, enter the appropriate information and click the 'Join Elance' button. The payment type you that choose in this step will become your default payment method and will be used to pay your monthly membership fee.

After all of this, you will be directed to start and work on your profile that describes who you are and what skills you offer. That is a very important step in the whole process and you should be getting ready with it before you even start the sign up process. You can continue to add additional information to your profile by clicking the 'Edit' button next to each section.

The next step is the fact that Elance.com has a test called Admission Test that you have to pass to be an Elance provider. The purpose of that test is to make sure that you understand how the whole system works on Elance.com. There are some complicated steps especially when start dealing with clients that you must fully understand. So, that test is free and it is in your favor. So before you even sign up, you need to on every piece of information on Elance.com and make sure you understand it. The admission test that you must pass, covers basic concepts of using Elance.com and shows that you understand how the Elance system works before engaging with potential employers.

The last step is to verify your phone number. To ensure that your information is accurate and up-to-date a valid phone number is required for all providers. Go to

Elance.com to learn more about how your phone will be verified. Your phone number will not be shared with third parties without your explicit consent and will only be used by Elance.com for the following purposes:

To contact you for questions or issues related to a job on Elance.com.

For any customer support matters related to your account.

For occasional input on the Elance.com platform and initiatives.

Once you select the type of the skill and you found a job or project you want to bid on, it is time to create what is called a proposal for that job. Creating effective proposals is crucial to your success. In your proposal you need to stress that you are uniquely qualified for that type of project and you understand the job or project requirements. You need to talk about your past experience in doing this kind of work. Providing few samples of your most recent work will help a lot. Then give a brief background. If you have questions don't be afraid to ask the client by using the Public Q&A Forum provided by Elance.com.

When it comes to the bidding process, be fair to your client and to yourself. You can't charge too much if you are just new or this is your first project on Elance.com. Try to spell everything in your proposal step by step. Make sure that your client knows exactly what you are going to do.

There are two fees associated with becoming an Elance provider:

Membership Fees: Elance.com offers monthly free and paid membership plans. All plans allow you to create a searchable profile and submit proposals to jobs in your skill category. There are four types of membership. You are only concerned with basic or fee membership.

Service Fee: For Elance.com providers who have a basic or free membership, the service fee is 6% plus 2.75% for payment processing.

When a job is awarded on Elance.com, a workroom is automatically created to manage the work. The workroom enables service providers and clients to work together safely and effectively, to communicate with each other in real time, share files, hold live meetings, automatically store important communication, make job status and progress visible at all times, eliminate paper work and ensure payments for results. To access a job workroom, log into your Elance account, click the Manage tab, click 'My Jobs' link and select the appropriate workroom by clicking on the job name.

Elance.com can help you manage hourly jobs. The Elance Work System provides a simple, streamlined process for clients and providers to negotiate hourly terms, report and invoice logged hours and approve and pay time sheets. For more information about that matter, go to Elance.com.

AS a service provider on Elance.com you can submit proposals on jobs on a specific service category. Elance.com has a search engine that ranks the Elance service providers according to certain criteria. The first one is the keywords you enter in your profile and the second one is your total earnings in the last 6 months on Elance.com. When you enter a keyword in your profile, Elance search engine first identifies all the provider profiles that match, then ranks the results by revenue and provider 'Reputation'. If two or more profiles appear to have identical relevance to your search, then the provider profiles with more Elance 'Reputation Score' are ranked higher in the search results. The following factors determine the match and ranking process:

Match: A match is determined by the presence of relevant skills and keywords withen the provider profile and within the provider's work history on Elance.com

Reputation: A member's reputation on Elance.com magnifies the match score and therefore determines the order in which profiles are displayed. The reputation on Elance.com is based on relevant and current performance and activity indicators. These indicators include the number of jobs completed, the quality of feedback received and the amount earned.

Displaying credentials e.g. education, awards, certificates etc. on your profile page is a great way to demonstrate your experience and expertise. Elance providers are encouraged to list credentials earned including certifications, professional licenses, degrees and references to previous employment on their provider profile as a way to illustrate their skills and expertise. You can have them verified for a fee ($15.00 for US based credentials at http://www.justifacts.com)

Feedback is an important part of working on Elance.com. Providers build a reputation of client satisfaction and employers build a history of consistent hiring and payment. These serve as references for both parties when evaluating who to work with in the future. Feedback can only be left by past clients and providers that have worked together on Elance.com,so you can be confident the work history is from the legitimate experiences of other Elance members.

Chapter 91

Making Money with Craigslist

When it comes to free local classifieds, nothing comes even closer to Craigslist. Craigslist can be a huge marketplace, not just in America but in the whole world. Anyone with an Internet access anywhere in the world can post free ads. This is a big chance for you to make money.

In Craigslist there are numerous categories and almost unlimited number of subcategories. The main categories are: Community, Personals, Discussion Forums, Housing, For sale, Jobs, Services, gigs, resumes. Go on these categories one by one and try to find out how you can make money using each one of them. You can advertise almost anything. To make good use of Craigslist, post your ads locally especially if you are selling something. I saw a lot of ads trying to advertise web sites which is not right on Craigslist. Most of the postings are free and you should take advantage of this.

<u>Posting Free Ads</u>

The first thing is to set up a free account. To do this, go to http://www.craigslist.org/login/signup. After you fill up the required information, you will be sent an e-mail that contains a link. The reason is to verify that you are legitimate owner of that e-mail. When you click on that link, it will take you to another web page where you type in a password. Once you have entered a password of your choice, click on 'Submit Password and Login' button. Review the Terms of use on the next page, then click 'I Accept' button if you agree with it. You are now logged into your account. To submit or post something, select your city from the drop down menu at the upper right and click the 'Go' button. The information you will be filling is straight forward. It is very important to enter a proper title in the Posting Title field because this is what people will click on to see the details of your posting description. When it comes to leaving a contact information for your posting, you have two choices. You can either give your e-mail address or your phone number. The problem with Craigslist is the fact that because it is global, there are lots of scams. That is why I never post my phone number. Although your e-mail address will not be visible on the web site and the responses you get will be forwarded to your e-mail account, I do not put my private e-mail. I just go and get a Yahoo e-mail and I use it specifically for Craigslist and other free classifieds. Once you have completed all the required fields, click 'Continue' at the bottom. You will be taken to a review screen of what your post will look like. If you need to make changes, click 'Edit'. When everything looks the way you want it, click 'Continue'. Your post will appear on the site in approximately 15 minutes. You can edit and delete your posting at anytime from your account page. Currently, you can add pictures to your post in the Housing, For Sale and Personals categories by selecting 'Add/Edit Images' at the bottom of the posting form.

Your posting should have an expiration date depending on the category. However, you can repost again. You may post to one category and in one city, no more often than about 48 hours. If you are submitting a post that is similar to another currently active post of yours on the site, you get a blocked message. You can't post your ad on more than one Craigslist site. Choose just one Craigslist site for which your ad is most relevant-this should generally be the site closest to where you are located. Posting the same ad to multiple locations is considered spamming and is prohibited. Generally, you can't put a link in your for sale posting pointing to an auction site like eBay and you can't post ads on Craigslist on behalf of others as a paid posting agent or posting service.

To summarize, you can use Craigslist to make money both locally, nationally and even on a global level. The best thing to do is to go to the site, http://www.Craigslist.org, and see how people are using it. You will be getting a lot of ideas and you will be amazed. Just do not forget the pen and the piece of paper. You can sell, promote your business and even make a lot of contacts. All of this is for free. The price is right!!

Chapter 92

Making Money with Free Classifieds

Imagine that you have something to sell or you are looking for a job and you can post your ad for free in hundreds of web sites. You can post your ad either locally or on the national level. It used to cost hundreds of dollars to post an ad in a magazine or a newspaper. No more! Life is much better now!

You can take advantage of the situation and make some money for yourself. If you have something to sell, you can post your free ad and start selling. If you have some kind of a skill and you want to do small jobs on the side, you can post your free ad to advertise your skill and try to grab some jobs. If you have a business and you have some vacancies to fill, you can post your free ad and fill up these jobs. There are unlimited ideas for how you can make money with these free classifieds. Some web sites even offer to help you with the design of your ads. Other web sites offer you some tips about how to design good effective ads.

There are hundreds of web sites that are offering free classifieds. I went through most of them to bring you the best in this book in an effort to save you the time and energy.

Google Base: I talked about Google base in a previous chapter. I do not want to repeat myself. You can go and read about it. All I can tell you here is that it is one of the best. That is why I mention it first.

Http://www.kijiji.com: This site belongs to eBay and it should be very good. For me it looks like Craigslist. It covers all US states and big cities. It is offering free local classifieds.

Http://www.ablewise.com: This web site looks decent to me. You can post free classifieds in different categories. You need to register first.

Http://Laclass.com: This is a great web site dedicated for the state of Louisiana. You can post your ad for free. You can even create your own ad for free. You can modify or erase your ad at any time.

Http://www.411classifieds.com: Looks a great web site. You need to sign up first before posting any free ads.

Http://www.cngnetwork.com: This web site looks great but you can't post any free ads. The reason I mentioned it is just to show you what an affiliation web site looks like. It is a collection of links to other web sites. When visitors click on these links, the web site makes money.

Http://www.1ads.com: It is a great web site. You can post free classifieds in different categories. You don't even have to sign up.

Http://www.pennysaverusa.com: It is a good site. It is offering free online classified ads in USA in a lot of categories. You need to sign in first. The site offers other paid services.

Http://www.netnickel.com: It offers free classified ad system for Southeastern Washington and Northeastern Oregon. Ads with a photo are free. It is a decent site.

Http://www.usfreeads.com: provides high traffic high response free classifieds since 1999. You have to sign up for an account. They have a knowledge base about how to sell, how to buy etc. They offer local classifieds in states and big US cities. I rate it as a good site.

Http://www.1second.com: This web site has two types of ads free or prime. Prime classified ads are located first and you have to pay to post in this category. Free classifieds are located in the last page of each category.

Http://www.theadnet.com: This is a web site where you can place your ad for free. You need to register first. Ads are free in most categories and run for 30 days. There is a nominal fee to place ads in Business opportunities, Employment and Services. Paid ads run for 90 days. It is generally considered a good site.

Http://www.photoads.co.uk: This web site is dedicated to post free ads for England. It is great if you want to do business in England.

Http://www.classifiedscentral.com: It offers free ads to only New York, Los Angeles, California, Texas and Florida. The site looks good but there are few ads there.

There are lots of other sites that let you post free classifieds. You can check them out whenever you have time.

Chapter 93

Making Money with your Online Store

I can mention to you many reasons why I would rather have an online store than having a real physical store. The first reason of course is the cost. It is much less expensive to start and maintain an online store than you can imagine. You do not need a start up money. You can cut on hiring. You can cut on other business expenses like rent, utilities, taxes, marketing etc. If you have a physical store you have you have to update your printed catalog on a weekly or monthly basis and this can cost a lot of money. But with an online store your catalog is always current with just a click of a mouse. If you have a physical store you can open only for many hours a day, but with an online store you are always open. People can order from your store while you are asleep. With a physical store your customers are mainly those living in your town or city. With an online store, the whole world is your customers.

It doesn't take too much time to start your online store and get it running. A physical store will take a lot of time for planning and executing. With an online store, there is an easy exit. If you fail you will not lose too much. You learn from the experience and you can start something better. With a physical store, if you fail it will be very hard to stand on your feet again. And I can give a lot more reasons.

Once you decide on having your online store, you need to start looking for a good company that can host your store. That is the hardest part. There are thousands of companies that are currently competing for your business. The competition is very tough and this is great for the consumers. Prices are down and services are better. A lot of these companies are offering free trial but do not be fooled with this. Once you are stuck with a company it will be hard to move to someplace else. So, what is really needed is to do your homework from the beginning and choose a winner. I can't recommend a certain company for you but you need to look for a company that is offering unlimited traffic just in case your business grows up. And you need a company with an excellent track record when it comes to customer service and technical support because no matter how good you are, you always need help. I will mention some companies here as an example but this does not mean they are the best because I did try few of them. You have to look for yourself and take that matter seriously.

EBay Online Stores: This can be a good start. It is easy to create, reasonable prices, a lot of traffic but it is not a full e-commerce solution and you are at the mercy of the customers. If you get a lot of negative feedback eBay will shut you down. I mean you are not totally in control.

Http://smallbusiness.yahoo.com/ecommerce: They offer different plans. Merchant starter plan starts at $39.95 a month. They have 1.5% transaction fee and $50.00 set up fee. They offer you unlimited disk space, unlimited data transfer and a free domain. Yahoo is a good company but you still need to shop around.

Http://www.volusion.com: It is an all-in-one e-Commerce solution. You can try it for 14 days free. They offer free 24x7x365 live phone support and live help or chat. Everything is included. They offer free templates. They have all the tools you need to sell online combined into one search engine friendly shopping cart software solution. Also, they offer free setup.

Http://www.3Dcart.com: They offer one month free trial and a variety of plans starting with $19.99 per month for 50 products, 1 GB bandwidth, live phone, email and chat support. They have $99.00 setup fee.

Http://www.hostgator.com: They offer 45 days money back guarantee, free templates, unlimited disk space, unlimited bandwidth and shared SSL Certificates for plan that starts at $4.95 a month.

Chapter 94

Making Money with Free Online Stores

Before you go and start building your real online store, I recommend that you start first by building a free online store. This can be a good learning experience for you before you get to the hard one.

There are many web sites that are offering free online stores but you need to remember that these web sites are not there to help you. They are there to make money. So there is always a catch. You need to figure out what the catch is for each one of these companies. Some of them offer you a free primitive online store in the hope that you upgrade in the future and be a paying customer and this is a good thing. In this case there is no catch. It is a very good way to get yourself into the e-Commerce world because you will learn a lot then you will be ready to start your own real store.

Here are some of the web sites that are offering free online stores. There is a lot more. Just go to any search engine and search for free online stores. You will get a long list that you need to go through each one of them. Pick up few two or three and start experimenting with them.

Http://www.Vendio.com

Http://www.1FreeCart.com

Http://www.MunCum.com

Chapter 95

Making Money with ClickBank

ClickBank.com claims that their clients have earned over one billion dollars so far. While I can't verify this claim, that is a huge amount of money and you can take your share of it. Practically, ClickBank.com offers two programs; one for vendors and the second is for the affiliates.

Vendors Program: It works this way. Suppose you are good in cooking and you want to share your experience with others and turn your hobby into profit at the same time. You create a new e-book called 'Cooking made simple' then you create a simple web site to promote your e-book but you need a way to attract customers and accept payments. You find out that ClickBank.com offers order processing, fraud protection and customer support for digital products like your e-book. ClickBank.com has more than 100,000 active affiliate marketers ready to promote your e-book. With ClickBank.com you are in control. You work with ClickBank.com to set the retail price and the affiliate commission for the e-book which you submit to ClickBank.com for approval. ClickBank.com quickly approves your product and you pay a one-time $49.95 activation fee. Your e-book is now live in the ClickBank Market Place and available for ClickBank affiliates to promote. ClickBank.com pays you and your affiliates automatically for each sale that occurs, giving you time and money to create your next great product.

Although ClickBank.com allows a huge variety of products, there are a few basic criteria that all products need to meet. All products must be original or appropriately licensed and can't infringe on the intellectual property of others. All products must be delivered to customers digitally via web pages, downloadable files or e-mail within 24 hours of purchase. Immediate delivery is preferred. Once you have created your first product, you may soon want to add more products. You can sell up to 500 products (or versions of the same product) in your account. However, in your account you may set only a single commission rate that applies to all of your products in that account and you have to use the same HopLink Target URL (the page where affiliates send traffic) for all products In that account. If you wish to sell very different types of products or offer varying commission rates, you can open a new account and in this case you pay a discounted fee of $29.95 because you have already the full $49.95 activation fee for your first vendor account. ClickBank.com can help you go global with your product. It makes it easy for you by allowing you to sell products in English, French, Spanish and German. In addition, ClickBank.com can accept payments in 13 different currencies which appeals to your customers and makes purchasing easier for them. ClickBank.com requires that your digital product or service to be provided in the language specified. It is also recommended that your product pitch page be presented in that language to reduce customer confusion and ultimately prevents high returns and charge backs. During product setup, vendors specify a default currency for their product. ClickBank.com will then present the product in the specified default currency for customers in geographic locations that utilize that currency. Customers from other geographic locations will see a converted currency most appropriate for their location. This flexibility increases the likelihood of making a sale by allowing vendors to specifically target their audience, while still allowing all potential buyers to make purchases in their local currency. All transactions are converted to USD and applied to your account at the time of purchase. The exchange rate is updated daily.

Choosing the right price for your product can be one of the most difficult but important decisions you make as a vendor. Unfortunately, there is no guaranteed way to ensure you have chosen the right price. There are some guidelines to help you. Search the ClickBank Market Place for similar products in your niche so you can see the normal range of pricing for that type of product. Your next step is to know the real value of your product and convince more affiliates to promote it. Don't price your product too low. One of the best ways to drive sales of your product is to make sure that affiliates want to promote it. Since many affiliates spend their time and money to promote your product, they need to make sure the return is worth. On the other hand, don't price your product too high. If you are just starting out, setting a high price can scare off potential customers unless your pitch page does a great job of selling them on the value of your product. High priced products may also lead to more refunds.

As soon as your product is approved and goes live, you will receive an e-mail notifying you whenever a sale of your product occurs.

Part of being a product vendor is that no matter how great your product is, you will occasionally receive return requests. ClickBank.com tries to make it as easy and painless as possible to handle these requests and attempt to save the sale. On your part, you need to do your best to prevent this from happening in the first place. Make sure that any claims on your pitch page are realistic and you have met expectations of your clients regarding your product. Respond properly to any customer support request. When you become a ClicBank vendor, the most difficult aspects of e-Commerce are taken care of for you, so you can concentrate on creating great products.

Selling your digital product through ClickBank.com is one of the best ways to quickly get exposure and sales for your product. Within a few business days you can be up and running and you have your product promoted by the huge network of affiliates. Here are the easy steps for getting setup as a ClickBank.com Vendor:

1. Sign up for a ClickBank.com account.
2. Create a pitch page and a thank you page. To sell a product through ClickBank.com you will need your own web site, including web hosting and a registered domain name. You can't sell a product through ClickBank using a web page hosted on free sites and ClickBank doesn't provide hosting for web pages or assistance with design or coding of web sites. The pitch page is used to describe your product to potential customers and convince them to buy. When your customers are ready to buy, they click on a ClickBank payment link on your pitch page that links them to the ClickBank Order Form where customers can place their order. The thank you page is the page customers will see after they purchase your product. Customers will only see this page if their purchase has been approved and the payment processed.
3. Make a Payment Link: When a customer is on your pitch page and ready to buy your product, you need to provide them with 'payment link' that sends them to the ClickBank Order Form where they can enter the payment information and complete the transaction. Once the payment is approved the customer is taken to a page hosted by ClickBank that confirms their order by providing them with a unique receipt number. Customers are then prompted to click a final link that takes them from this confirmation page to your thank you page where you provide them with clear instructions on how to download or access

the product or information on how and when it will be delivered to them. You will need to manually create a payment link to send customers to the order form and then insert this payment link in HTML code on your pitch page.

4. Complete My Site Information within your account. The first thing is to designate a HopLink Target URL. One of the biggest benefits of being a ClickBank vendor is having access to a huge affiliate network. Affiliates advertise vendors' products by enticing visitors to click on their affiliate link (also known as a HopLink) and hop over to your pitch page to make a purchase. The first step to take advantage of this affiliate network is specifying the URL where affiliates should send potential customers. Typically it is the same URL as your pitch page. After you have designated a HopLink Target URL, fill out details about your product to display in the ClickBank Market Place. An accurate and compelling Market Place description will help affiliates find your product and can convince them to promote it.

5. Complete My Products Information within your account. To enter important information about your product such as location of your thank you page, your suggested retail price etc.

6. Test your payment link. Before submitting your product for approval you must go through the process of purchasing your product as if you were a customer. That way you can make sure that all of your links are working properly before potential customers visit you.

7. Request product approval. Before you can start setting your product with ClickBank.com it needs to be approved by ClickBank's Approval Team. Once you have completed the steps above, you can submit a Product Approval Request.

8. Pay a one-time $49.95 Activation Charge. Once you receive the approval e-mail for your first product, you will need to pay your one-time $49.95 Activation Charge. Once your product is activated, it will be listed in the ClickBank Market Place and ready for affiliates to promote. You can also begin accepting orders through the ClickBank Order Form.

ClickBank.com has a huge network of over 100,000 active affiliates who can promote your product. Affiliates regularly search the Market Place for interesting new products to promote. An affiliate sees your product and decides to promote it. They advertise it in many different places online using a variety of paid and free promotional techniques such as writing about it in their blog or paying for advertising on search engines. Their efforts drive potential customers to your pitch page, where customers read about your product and decide to buy.

After the sale is processed, ClickBank.com receives its transaction processing charges, ClickBank.com receives its transaction processing charges (7.5% plus $1.00) then pays the affiliate commission percentage (which you choose) based on the remaining amount. The rest of the money goes to you. If no affiliate drives the sale, you keep the entire amount after processing charges. The easiest way to get affiliates to promote your product is to list in the ClickBank Market Place with a compelling description. Also, offering a generous commission percentage (that can be as high as 75%).

Affiliates Program: It works this way. If you think about starting making money online, you go to ClickBank.com to sign up for a free account. Now you are ready to promote digital products. You can visit the ClickBank Market Place and have instant access to tens of thousands of products available for promotion. No contracting or waiting. If it happens that you find something you like e.g. the e-book about cooking, within seconds you can create a personalized HopLink to promote. After this, you go online to post your HopLink in search engines ads and in your blog and in the e-book review you wrote for your favorite cooking forum and so on. Your hard work pays off a now ClickBank.com pays you your commission (up to 75% of the sale) for each time someone clicks on your Hoplink and buys the e-book. You can go back to the Market Place and choose other products to promote (as many as you want). This way your earnings grow. There is no charge for affiliates to sign up. There is no limit to the number of products you can promote.

Becoming a ClickBank.com affiliate is a quick and easy process.

1. Create an account: Once you create an account, you will have your Account Home Page. This is the page where you will be able to see your earnings as well as important ClickBank news, updates and more.

2. <u>Find a product to promote:</u> The best place to start is the ClickBank Market Place. Once you have selected a product, click create Hoplink below the product listing.

3. <u>Start promoting your HopLinks:</u> You do not need a web site to be a ClickBank affiliate but if you have one it can be a great place to promote your HopLinks. The number of ways to promote the products is nearly unlimited. You can write articles and submit them to different web sites and blogs then you post your HopLink so you get credit if someone ends up purchasing the product. Once you identified a niche market that you want to promote e.g. cooking, you create your own web site or blog that is dedicated to that topic. Then you write articles for your own web site. The goal is to get free traffic to your web site either by getting linked from other web sites or by ranking high by different search engines. Then you can have your HopLinks to a number of different ClickBank.com products in that niche. You can also use social media marketing. The key to being successful promoting products in the social media space is to provide content that is worthwhile enough for people to actually want to follow you and take your advice when you recommend products. Finally you can use search engine optimization and pay per click advertising.

Unlike some other affiliate networks, ClickBank.com handles all sales processing and commission tracking so vendors can't attempt to avoid paying commission on sales. As a ClickBank.com affiliate one of the first things you need to know is how to use HopLinks to promote ClickBank.com products. There is a lot of information on ClickBank.com about how to create them and how to use them. An important part of being a successful affiliate is tracking your promotional efforts so you can know what is working for you and what is not. The first place you will want to look at is ClickBank's transactions reporting. Seeing how many people are clicking your HopLinks compared to the number of sales you are receiving is an important first step in understanding what products are performing well. If you promote products using your own web site, it is extremely helpful to install some sort of web analytics so you can see how many visitors you are getting and how they interact with your web site. There are a wide variety of options the most popular of which are Google Analytics and Yahoo Web Analytics. Both are free, easy to use and quick to install.

Chapter 96

Making Money with RentAcoder.com

This site simply brings two people together and closes the deal. If you have something needs to be done you just go to RentAcoder.com and solicit bids on the job. There are thousands of registered coders on the RAC web site, some of them are ready to bid on your job. If you have a high tech skill you can earn cash with it. On the other hand, if you need a custom software or a web site fix or other related job you can receive bids on it. RentAcoder.com offers two things connected together. You can make money as a software coder and you can save money as a software buyer.

<u>Software Coders:</u>

Software coders are generally these people who have technical computer skills, skills related to the Internet and web sites and writing skills in general. These skills are in high demand and you can make a lot of money by doing small projects and quick fixes that clients (RentAcoder.com calls them software buyers) request on RAC web site. The term software is actually misleading because most of the requested work is not actually programming. It is just simple things. You do not need to be a software engineer to bid on these small projects. Actually most of these projects or assignments can be done by a high school kid who is crazy about computers. So do not let that term scare you.

If you feel this opportunity is for you, the first thing to do is to register in the site. Registration is free. As soon as you register you can cash in on your areas of expertise. RentAcoder.com automatically notifies you of new programs or questions in your area of interest and expertise. You can then bid on the ones you are interested in. After the customer accepts your bid, you create the program or answer the questions. When you are finished you are awarded the bid amount. RentAcoder.com generally charges coders 15% of the final bid. This fee covers buyer advertising, buyer credit card / PayPal processing, security verification of buyer payments, facilitation/ arbitration, site costs and small profit. The RAC fee is reduced for different auction types and / or if the buyer uses a preferred payment method. Additionally, on very small projects, there is a minimum fee of $3.00. The RAC fee and your end profit are conveniently calculated and displayed for you whenever you confirm a bid. A preferred method of payment works this way. When a buyer sends a payment via a means that is less expensive for RAC to accept and process, RAC passes the savings on to you. When a buyer uses a bank to bank wire transfer or mail a check to escrow all of the funds for the bid request the winning coder receives a RAC fee reduction of 2.5%. This can be a great way to make some extra money with very little extra effort. After the buyer accepts your bid, his money is held in an escrow account. After you deliver the product and they acknowledged that they received everything or sign off on your time card, you will be credited with the escrow amount minus the RAC finders fee. You can choose to have the payments sent to you via a number of methods.

In compliance with the IRS rules, all US coders who make $600.00 in a year receive an IRS 1099 form from RentAcoder.com. A copy is also sent to the IRS.

When you register with RAC, you make a registration profile for yourself. To promote yourself and make customers more likely to accept your bid, you should include in your profile a resume, list of areas of expertise and certifications, a sample of your portfolio, a personal photograph, a company logo etc.

As a coder RAC has some measures to protect you and ensure a fair transaction. First, you can instantly check the reputation of any customer who is posting a project. You can review their ratings (from 1 to 10) , read the feedback that previous programmers have left about them and other things. Read this carefully before deciding whether or not to make a bid. Second, by the time you begin work each customer has already prepaid the bill for the bid request and RentAcoder.com is already holding it in escrow. If you complete the work as specified you can be confident of being paid. Third, should you ever get into a dispute over what has been delivered with the buyer, you can enlist the help of a third party. Just place the bid into arbitration with a RAC arbitrator. They will determine what has actually been delivered (or not) and the buyer and yourself has already pre agreed to abide by their decision.

To communicate with the buyer or ask questions simply post a comment on the bid request. The buyer will be emailed a link to your posting and if he responds, you will receive an email of their response as well and so on.

Software Buyers:

These are the clients who have work to be done. Projects vary from small projects to very large ones. RAC allows you locate experienced programmers from around the world quickly and easily. You just enter your project or problem along with the maximum you are willing to pay and programmers will bid down the price in order to earn your business. You can save a lot of money this way. You can quickly view the qualifications and resume of each programmer who bids on your project as well as their approval ratings from previous customers.

There are no service charges or finder's fees for buyers. Registration is free and posting a bid request is free. You are under no obligation to accept any bids sent to you unless you choose to. After you accept a buyer's bid you submit the bid amount to an escrow account via credit cards, PayPal, postal mail check or bank to bank wire transfer. Only after you receive the deliverables and approve them, will be the escrowed funds be transferred to the coder. This guarantees that the coder will work his hardest to get you the results that you asked for. RAC has a number of features that make the site an easy and safe place to purchase coder related solutions and services.

Choosing a Coder:

To help you choose a coder, you can instantly check the reputations and history of all bidders. Ratings range from 1 to 10 (1 being the worst and 10 being the best). A comment log left by other buyers who have worked with the programmer in the past is also available. Additionally, if you feel uncomfortable and would like assistance in choosing the best coder for your situation, a RAC facilitator with experience in project management is available to assist you in choosing the best coder for your needs.

To guarantee that your coder is motivated and committed to completing your project, you can require that they place an Expert Guarantee. The coder deposits a certain amount of money (which the two of you can negotiate) into a deposit escrow. If they fully complete the project then they receive the deposit back . If they do not complete the project, then they lose some or all of the deposit. This is the best way to find a coder who is fully committed to your project.

If you need to protect trade secrets while selecting a coder, RAC offers a non-disclosure agreement feature for maximum protection of your intellectual property.

Working with a Coder:

RAC guarantees a stress free transaction by putting you in control of releasing funds to the coder. You do not pay the coder directly but instead deposit the funds into an escrow account. Upon completion of the work (or work phase) you verify that you have received what you have asked for and authorize the release of funds through the site. Since you are in control, you can guarantee that you will get the deliverables that you are asking for. Once your bid is accepted you receive the coder's email information and may exchange phone numbers, addresses etc at both parties discretion. In addition to this, weekly coder status reports keep you updated (required only if coder is working on projects over $150.00). That way if coder is running into problems or getting off course, you will know right away rather than it is too late. If you find yourself in a dispute with the coder you can put the bid into arbitration with a RAC arbitrator. They will determine what has actually been delivered and the coder and yourself has already pre agreed to abide by their decision. If it turns out is unable or unwilling to do the work, you can switch to another coder at no charge.

The best way to choose a coder depends on whether or not you have a deadline that you need your project finished by. If you have a deadline (more money than time) then the single most important criterion in evaluating a coder is his experience on the site followed by his job skills. The number one mistake that inexperienced buyers with time frames make is picking the cheapest coder. This generally means the coder has no work experience or history on the site and there is a chance that he will not meet your deadline. So if your timeline is important, don't make this mistake. If you have no deadline (more time than money) then time is on your side and you should strongly consider taking a chance on a coder with little or no experience on the site. You can generally get quite a discount this way and you can do it safely.

Affiliate Program:

RentAcoder.com offers a very generous affiliate program. For every new buyer that you refer RAC gives you one third of the profits. This is more than any other site on the net. To prevent fraud, the profits are calculated when the project is completed and accepted by the buyer as complete. You are paid only for new buyers that are referred and only for their first project on the site. Affiliates will not be paid for projects from buyers who are already members. Becoming an affiliate is absolutely free. Once you have earned over $500.00 in affiliate fees, you are eligible to apply for the super affiliate program and earning a whooping of 50% of the profits on your referrals. All the payments are handled the same way that software coder payments are handled.

Chapter 97

VOIP WEB SITE

VOIP stands for Voice Over the Internet Protocol. It is a very hot topic these days and for generations to come. VOIP has great benefits for both individuals and businesses. It is actually considered indispensable technology in a lot of companies and businesses. Why VOIP is in such a high demand these days. Here are some of the reasons:

1. COST: VOIP can save you a lot of money. The calls are very cheap. Some calls can be free of charge. You can save a lot on international and long distance calls. Some companies reported saving about 75% on their international calls. That is a lot of savings. There are three ways in which users can make use of VOIP services: PC to PC (good example of this is Windows Live Call Software, Gizmo and Skype where you can call anywhere in the world for free), Phone to PC or PC to Phone calls and Phone to Phone calls. In these latter two you pay a minimum charge but overall you save a lot of money.
2. It is great for professionals who are always on the go. They can use their wireless Internet Connection and a VOIP telephone ready to make their calls for a very cheap price.
3. VOIP can help you arrange real time audio and even video conferencing at a very cheap price. So there is no need for face to face meeting and you save on travelling expenses.
4. It can be easily integrated with your network and email. This will enhance productivity.

There is a lot to do with VOIP. The question is where you fit in all of this and how you can make money with a VOIP web site. There are three approaches. The first approach is very simple. Build your own web site. Write a lot of articles about VOIP. How it works, devices you need, the leaders in the industry and so on. The content of your web site should be distinguished and of high value or you will not get any traffic. Then you start getting advertising from the big three Google, Yahoo and Microsoft. This can be a great source of revenue. The second way of making money is to find the top leaders in this new technology and affiliate with them. This way you make even more money through affiliations.

The second approach is to build a web site dedicated to what is called reseller programs. You create a VOIP reseller program where you resell and market VOIP phone service and generate a commission from the sale. A lot of VOIP vendors are offering these reseller programs. You can approach one or two companies and contract with them. Your job is to get them more subscribers and in turn you earn more commission.

A third approach is to join what is called wholesale VOIP where you sell complete package solutions of VOIP telephony. This usually needs more resources and you will be mainly dealing with businesses. The reward can be very great. This usually will include everything that is involved in migrating from a traditional phone system to a VOIP phone system. It will include planning, installation, consulting etc. You can search the Internet for companies offering VOIP wholesaling programs. There are lots of them. You need to carefully choose your providers to get the best deals out of the program. There is usually a one-time setup fee to start the business. Look for a company that offers a lot of training and support. Should you succeed in this last approach you can very easy make millions of dollars in sales every year.

Chapter 98

Web Site for Network Security

Though the field of network security is currently overloaded, there is still more room for other players. The topic is so important today and for years to come.

This web site idea is very simple. You are not going to program anything or write any code. You are not going to sell any security software either. The only way to make money with this web site is to have a great content to attract traffic then make money through advertising and affiliations. In addition to attracting a lot of audience, good content will help you achieve a top ranking among different search engines and this way you can attract even more audience. Try to Link to every web site that has great content about network security. Also, do your best to Write a lot of good articles about network security and post them in your web site. You can ask other people to contribute and post good articles to your web site. Your web site should be the encyclopedia of network security on the web. You need to talk about how important network security is. You need to talk about computer viruses, spywares, hackers etc. You need to talk about the measures that people should use to protect their computers and networks. You can offer some of the tools that help people check for free if their computers are working properly or not. Find out if you can provide these tools for free to your audience visiting your web site. Remember that you have to offer something for free to attract traffic.

After creating that great web site with that great content that will attract traffic, it is time to think about making money with this site. The first option for you is advertising. The big advertising companies are Google, Yahoo and Microsoft. You can apply for any one of them or all of them. The second option is to find out the companies that are offering network security solutions and join their affiliate programs. This way you can have two lucrative sources of revenue.

In the beginning, it will take too much time and hard work to setup such a web site. Once you web site is up and running, you do not have to do a lot of work. But you have to keep update with what is new in the field and the job of marketing your site will never end. You have to do a lot of marketing and find out new ideas and ways of marketing your web site. With hard work, your efforts will pay off.

Chapter 99

Web Site for Security Systems

Security is a very big issue these days and it will be even more important in the future. Our resources are limited and the world population is increasing rapidly. If this trend continues, there will be a lot of problems, more crimes and more security lapses all over the world. That is why a lot of companies are developing all kinds of security systems for home, businesses, offices, government buildings and so on. On your web site, you can't sell all of this. You need to pick up one sector like home security systems or business security systems. You can also sell security gadgets for personal use. You need first to find out what is available. Make a long list of what is available in the market concerning security. If you do a good thorough research you will find thousands of products that you can sell. It will take time to settle on what you are going to sell. You need to have your own online catalog and you need to include as many products as you can in this catalog. This can make your site a great source for security products. Every product should have its own web page with a lot of details about the product, a lot of good pictures, price and shipping information. Of course, you will need a shopping cart and some sort of payment processing system. You need to include a lot of articles about security systems and why everybody needs them. The more articles you have the better your web site will be. This arrangement alone can be a great source of revenue for you.

You can include advertising in your web site to generate even more revenue. If you can't sell products on your web site for whatever reasons, the alternative for you is to affiliate with the companies that are currently selling these security systems. This way you can generate another source of revenue.

You need to follow the rules for designing a good web site so you can attract more customers.

Chapter 100

Today's Funny Web Site

Life is full of stress. There are lots of stressful situations that we have to face in our daily lives whether we are rich or poor. So, we all need to relax and be entertained. That is why we have a surge in web sites that are filled up with jokes, funny things and funny videos.

You will be doing better when you create a funny web site if you are a funny person yourself and if you like to have a good time and you are good with people. This will be a dream business for you as you will be able to make money and have fun at the same time.

The first thing that your web site should have is the best joke of the day. It is your job everyday to go and search the Internet, select the best joke then post it in your web site for your audience. You need to mention the source and to find out whether or not you need a permission to post it. It is very important to follow the copy rights rules. Ask your audience about their opinions. Make an archive for all the jokes so people can go back and have a look at them.

The second thing to add to your web site is the funniest video clip of the day. Find the funniest video on the web from your standpoint of view and post it to your web site.

You can also add other things like strange situations funny stories etc. Also, you can post articles with great eye catching titles like you can be funny too, how to relax, kill stress and so on. Good articles are a great way to build huge audience.

You need to be very active in social networking sites like FaceBook.com and MySpace.com

This is very important. How to market your web site using social networking sites is an essential step that you should take seriously. There is a huge audience in these web sites for what you have in your web site and you can take advantage of this.

You can make a lot of money advertising. You can have Google ads, Yahoo ads or Microsoft ads. You can make a lot of money just from advertising because I expect you will have a lot of traffic. Another thing is to affiliate with companies selling items that help people deal with stress, improve their mental health etc. There are lots of companies that are offering for example seminars or courses to deal with stress. You can affiliate with companies that are offering vacation packages and the possibilities are unlimited. You can continuously think about other ways to boost your income.

Visit other web sites that are doing the same thing and see what they are doing. Not only you will be able to copy their success but you will also be able to have the competitive advantage over them. Always look for the competitive advantage. This will give you an edge over your competition and translate into more traffic and more revenue.

CONCLUSION

This book comes to an end. I hope you can find something in this book that can change your life for the best. My advice is to read the book more than once and take some notes for what makes sense to you.

The Internet is here to stay. It is a robust new technology that is shaking everything from banks to the postal service. You can feel the Internet Impact everywhere all over the globe. If you do not follow the Internet wave, you will be helpless and your chance of having a good future will be much in doubt.

It will pay to learn at least, the basics of computing, Internet business and Internet marketing. It will save you a lot of money if you learn web site design and development. This is the new revolution and you need to be part of it. You do not want to be left behind. In the future, most of the wealth will be created through things that have something to do with the Internet. So you better get your coat on before it is too late.